OSPREY
PUBLISHING

US Marine Co   ic
Theater of Ope
1943–44

Gordon L Rottman • Consultant editor Dr Duncan Anderson

Series editors Marcus Cowper and Nikolai Bogdanovic

First published in Great Britain in 2004 by Osprey Publishing, Elms Court,
Chapel Way, Botley, Oxford OX2 9LP, United Kingdom.
Email: info@ospreypublishing.com

ISBN 1 84176 651 8

Editorial by Ilios Publishing, Oxford, UK (www.iliospublishing.com)
Design: Bounford.com, Royston, UK
Maps by Bounford.com, Royston, UK
Index by Fineline Editorial Services
Originated by The Electronic Page Company, Cwmbran, UK
Printed and bound by L-Rex Printing Company Ltd

04 05 06 07 08   10 9 8 7 6 5 4 3 2 1

A CIP catalog record for this book is available from the British Library.

FOR A CATALOG OF ALL BOOKS PUBLISHED BY OSPREY MILITARY
AND AVIATION PLEASE CONTACT:

Osprey Direct USA, c/o MBI Publishing, P.O. Box 1,
729 Prospect Ave, Osceola, WI 54020, USA
E-mail: info@ospreydirectusa.com

Osprey Direct UK, P.O. Box 140, Wellingborough,
Northants, NN8 2FA, UK
E-mail: info@ospreydirect.co.uk
www.ospreypublishing.com

Author's note

Many contemporary abbreviations and styles have been used in
this and the accompanying USMC volumes.

Abbreviated dates: these follow the style adopted in official
Marine histories and studies and in most other Marine-related
references, namely day/month/year.

Rank abbreviations: these too follow official Marine practice,
e.g. BGen (Brigadier-General), MajGen (Major-General), LtGen
(Lieutenant-General).

Marine division and brigade: these are frequently abbreviated
to MarDiv and MarBde respectively, following contemporary
practice.

Unit designations: Battalions organic to Marine regiments are
designated with the battalion and regimental number, for
example "1/7" for "1st Battalion, 7th Marines." Note also that
"7th (etc.) *Marines*" always refers to a Marine *regiment*, whereas
"4th Marine Division" is the correct way to list a Marine division:
this distinction serves to avoid any confusion between regiments
and divisions.

Companies and batteries are designated in a similar fashion, for
example "D/1/2" for "Company D, 1st Battalion, 2d Marines."
Army infantry regiments are designated "1/106 Infantry" for
"1st Battalion, 106th Infantry."

Commanders' dates: When multiple unit commanders are listed
for a unit, the date of the first commander is the date the unit
commenced participation in the operation and not the date he
assumed command. Officers shown as wounded in action (WIA),
but not followed by a replacing officer were returned to duty.

Unit trees and maps: In the unit tree diagrams and maps in
this volume, the USMC designation symbol has not been shown
throughout: unless otherwise indicated, all units are USMC,
and are olive drab color. US Army units are shown in mid-blue.
Japanese units and positions are shown in red. For a key to the
symbols used in this volume, see below.

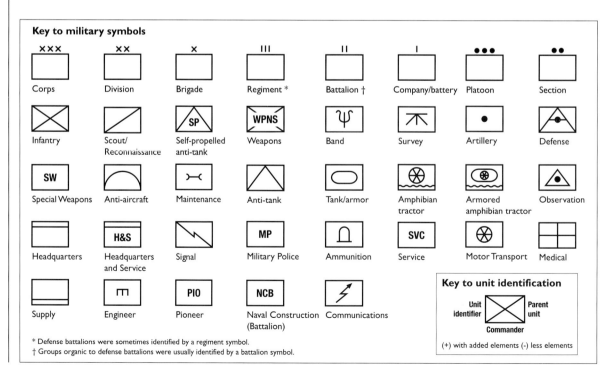

Contents

Introduction

The US Marine Corps (USMC) was one of three components of the wartime Navy Department, the others being the US Navy (USN) and US Coast Guard. On January 1, 1944 LtGen Alexander A. Vandegrift, former Commanding General, I Marine Amphibious Corps (IMAC), became the 18th Commandant of the Marine Corps, assuming the duty from LtGen Thomas Holcomb.

The USMC was subdivided into two broad organizations: the Fleet Marine Force (FMF); and the Shore Establishment, plus Headquarters, Marine Corps (HQMC) in Arlington Annex, Navy Department, Washington, DC. The FMF contained the Corps' operating elements: ground combat, aviation, service, and most training units. The Shore Establishment included Marine Corps schools, supply depots, recruiting stations, recruit training depots, and Marine barracks and detachments guarding naval bases, stations, and depots.

By January 1944 the Marine Corps had grown to 28,193 officers, 10,723 officer candidates, and 366,353 enlisted Marines, with a total of 405,169 personnel: of these, 10,430 were female. The FMF had grown to two amphibious corps, four divisions (with a fifth about to be activated), a separate infantry regiment, 19 defense battalions, and numerous support and service units: the total number of Marines and sailors in ground units was 199,324. Marine Aviation had grown to four aircraft wings, 21 groups, and 88 squadrons, totaling 91,075 personnel.

The Marine Corps' early-war organization and first offensive actions in the Solomons, on Guadalcanal, in the Russells, on New Georgia, and on Bougainville are covered in Battle Orders 1: *US Marine Corps Pacific Theater of Operations 1941–43*. At the end of December 1943, the final Marine operation in this Pacific area took place, on New Britain in the Bismarcks; a little earlier, in November 1943, the Corps' first operation in the Central Pacific on Tarawa had been executed. Both of these are covered in this book. Additional Marine operations conducted in the Central Pacific in 1944 included Roi-Namur, Eniwetok, Saipan, and Tinian. Three of the four existing Marine divisions participated in these operations. The organization of the 4th Marine Division (MarDiv) and III and V Amphibious Corps (IIIAC, VAC) is discussed along with smaller, new units.

The forthcoming Battle Orders 8: *US Marine Corps Pacific Theater of Operations 1944–45* will cover the formation of the 5th and 6th MarDivs along with the 1st Provisional Marine Brigade (Prov MarBde), from which the 6th was organized, and the final, brutal battles on Guam, Peleliu, Iwo Jima, and Okinawa. The organization and operations of Marine Corps Aviation, and the organization of raider and parachute units are the subject of future proposed titles in this series.

Battle-hardened Marines take charge of children on Saipan, as Japanese civilians turn themselves in. The civilians were told that the Marines would torture and kill them if taken alive: thousands tragically committed suicide as a result.

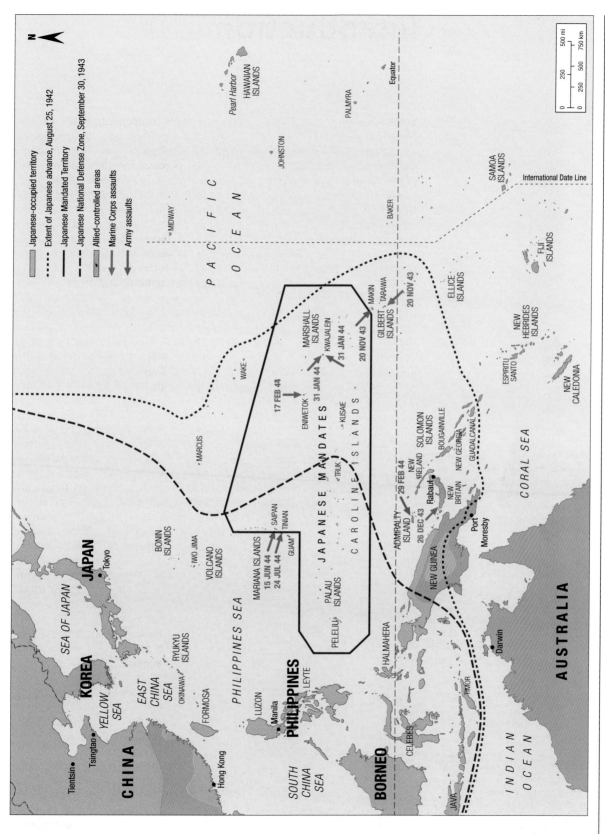

Strategic situation, Pacific Theater, 1943–44.

Combat mission

By the end of 1943 the Marine Corps had established itself as an extremely proficient amphibious assault force capable of landing a reinforced division on a hostile shore, supporting it, and defeating the enemy. The Corps had additional missions, ranging from defending advanced naval bases, garrisoning remote islands, amphibious reconnaissance, clandestine operations, ship and Stateside naval installation guard duty, training native militias and foreign troops, guarding embassies, and ceremonial duties. The war in the Pacific, where the Marines fought almost alone, had quickly become a joint campaign involving the US Navy and US Army as well as the air arms of all three services. The campaign also saw the participation of Australian, New Zealand, and British forces.

The Fleet Marine Force (FMF) was established in December 1933 to provide the Fleet with a force capable of expeditionary operations and advance naval base defense. It could seize and secure naval bases and defend existing overseas bases. This required a self-contained force with offensive ground combat units, defense units, aviation, and service elements capable of conducting joint operations. It was these early efforts that allowed the Corps to adjust and expand its capabilities to meet the needs of the Pacific War.

The Marine Corps was a comparatively small branch of service. At the beginning of 1944 the Army mustered over 5,286,000 personnel with an additional 1,811,000 soldiers in the Army Air Forces. The Navy had 2,381,000 with another 172,000 in the Coast Guard. At the beginning of 1944, the units in the Pacific Theater were the Sixth Army, I and XIV Corps, and 13 divisions. Two more army headquarters, three corps, and seven divisions would deploy to the Pacific in 1944. Of the 22 Army divisions that served in the Pacific, 18 conducted 26 major amphibious operations. The six Marine divisions conducted 17 major landings along with smaller landings.

Amid damaged LVT(2)s on Tinian, casualties are prepared for evacuation to troop transports. Two 5-gallon water cans and a gasoline can (note the different caps) can be seen in the foreground along with 81mm heavy HE mortar-round tubes.

Expanding the Marine Corps

Throughout 1943 the Marine Corps and Navy refined their amphibious doctrine and capabilities. New types of units were fielded to meet unforeseen requirements or to operate new weapons. Operations gradually became larger with amphibious corps conducting multi-division landings. Standardization of procedures became more widespread. There was still, however, much field experimentation, ad hoc provisions to meet specific tactical and logistical challenges, and a general lack of standardization between major commands. IIIAC and VAC would organize and operate very differently from each other. The 4th MarDiv had been activated in 1943, but would not see combat until 1944. The 5th and 6th MarDivs too were activated in 1944, but saw no combat until 1945. In 1944 the 1st–4th MarDivs were assigned the following units:

	1st MarDiv	2d MarDiv	3d MarDiv	4th MarDiv
Infantry regiments	1st, 5th, 7th	2d, 6th, 8th	3d, 9th, 21st	23d, 24th, 25th
Artillery Regiment	11th	10th	12th	14th
Engineer Regiment*	17th	18th	19th	20th
HQ Battalion	1st MarDiv	2d MarDiv	3d MarDiv	4th MarDiv
Medical Battalion	1st	2d	3d	4th
Motor Transport Battalion	1st	2d	3d	4th
Service Battalion	1st	2d	3d	4th
Tank Battalion	1st	2d	3d	4th

The engineer regiments were deactivated between May and September 1944. The engineer and pioneer battalions were retained and redesignated with their division's number.

Lessons learned in the Solomons in 1943 were integrated into training, tactics, weapons employment, and logistics. Extensive refinements in intelligence, communications, naval gunfire and air support control, operational planning, and supply levels were made. Newly raised units in the States exploited such lessons in their training and continued to do so as they moved to bases in Hawaii,

A portion of the 13 separate recruit battalions at Marine Barracks, Parris Island, South Carolina salute President Roosevelt in March 1943. The commander described the post's mission as follows: "We have but one principal wartime function: to be of service to the Marine Corps combat units. This is accomplished by giving basic training to thousands of recruits destined for our corps and division troops, by turning out trained cooks, bakers, bandsmen, trumpeters, drummers, motor vehicles drivers and mechanics, clerks, first sergeants, field telephone operators, field radio operators, and sea school graduates; by acting as school, depot, transport agent and hotel keeper for the Fleet Marine Force."

New and larger landing craft
By late-1943 large numbers of landing craft and ships were sent to the Pacific to greatly increase the landing of troops, weapons, vehicles, ammunition, and supplies. The earlier, limited-capacity beaching craft were replaced wholesale. The landing ship, tank (LST) and landing craft, infantry (LCI) were able to deliver large amounts of equipment and numbers of troops after crossing short distances of open sea.
The vehicle-landing ship equivalent of the LCI, the landing ship, medium (LSM), became available in 1944. The landing craft, tank (LCT) and a smaller version, the landing craft, mechanized (LCM), both provided in several marks, became common for delivering tanks, artillery, and vehicles. The small landing craft, vehicle or personnel (LCVP) soon replaced earlier versions of troop-landing craft to become the most widely used beaching craft.
The LST pictured above transports an LCT(5), which was launched by listing the LST to one side. Aboard the LCT are two Army MTL light tugs.

New Zealand, and the Solomons. Greatly improved amphibious warfare ships and landing craft also joined the fleet.

The garrisoning of South Pacific islands to secure the Southern Lifeline between America and Australia and New Zealand had been the major focus of the war's initial stage. The next stage comprised offensive operations into the Solomons to eliminate Japanese conquests, along with offensive operations in New Guinea. The Solomons gave the Allies the opportunity to establish air, naval, logistical, and staging bases from which to launch attacks to the north, into the Bismarck Archipelago and the Gilberts in the Central Pacific. Further operations in 1944 would see the seizure of the Marshalls, Marianas, and Carolines. These operations were conducted under Commander-in-Chief, Pacific Ocean Area, Adm. Chester W. Nimitz. This would be the Marine Corps' principal focus. In the Southwest Pacific Area, Gen. Douglas MacArthur conducted operations on New Guinea with the objective of liberating the Philippines: Marines would only play a peripheral role in these.

Further growth of the FMF

As US forces thrust into the Central Pacific at the beginning of 1944, the FMF continued to grow. Not only were combat and service units expanded, but so were training units and the supporting shore establishment. 1944 actually saw the peak strength of the Marine Corps, although some units had not yet been committed to combat. By the end of this year, the Corps possessed 42 infantry battalions in 18 regiments, 23 regimental and 11 separate artillery battalions, 3 defense, 12 anti-aircraft artillery, 6 tank, 9 amphibian tractor, 3 armored amphibian tractor, and 8 engineer battalions. Additionally, there were dozens of divisional and non-divisional headquarters, medical, military police, motor transport, service, and signal battalions. While the growth of the Corps had been rapid, far beyond the expectations of even 1942 projections, in some instances fewer units than planned were activated. The FMF Plan for Fiscal Year 1943 (July 1, 1943–June 30, 1944) projected more units than the Operating Force Plan eventually authorized. Units projected, but never raised, included 3 airdrome (AA), 8 defense, 1 anti-tank, 1 corps medium tank, 2 raider, and 1 separate infantry battalions.

Many of the personnel destined for these proposed units were used as replacements for the higher than expected casualties. The Marine Corps intended to remove personnel from the combat zone after 14 months, but the casualty rate, activation of new units, and the tempo of operations stretched this to 24–30 months. Personnel removed from the combat zone were assigned to Stateside training units, schools, service and administrative organizations, Marine barracks, and ships' detachments. Many, especially officers and NCOs, were reassigned to newly raised combat units to again deploy overseas.

Numerous provisional units were raised in the Pacific Theater. In 1944, there were 2,100 such troops in 20 provisional battalions, companies, and detachments. HQMC was concerned by the formation of these units, as the need for them was not always apparent, there was a tendency to retain them after the need had passed, and they prevented personnel from being assigned to regular units to allow troop rotation.

Between September 1942 and June 1944 replacements trained in the States were transferred to the Pacific Theater via the 1st–69th replacement battalions. Varying in size from a few hundred to over 1,000 troops, they were dispatched to specific divisions or corps for assignment to units by classification specialists. From July 1944 replacement drafts served as the means to transfer personnel. The increase in the tempo of operations demanded more replacements. The drafts, still organized similarly to a battalion, arrived with over 1,000 troops and sometimes up to almost 5,000. The 1st–81st replacement drafts were dispatched by the war's end.

Recruits received their training at Marine Corps recruit depots at Parris Island, SC or San Diego, CA. Specialty training was undertaken at Marine Corps training centers at Camp Lejeune, NC; Camp Elliott, CA; and Camp Pendleton, CA. Officer training took place at Marine Barracks, Quantico, VA. Marine bases and training activities in southern California were extensive and were under the control of FMF, San Diego Area from 1942. Training organizations were consolidated under Marine Training Command, FMF, San Diego Area in June 1944. Besides the bases at San Diego, Elliott, and Pendleton, other large camps were established in the area to include Camp Kearny for unit housing and training, Camp Robert H. Dunlap for artillery ranges, Camp Gillespie for parachute training, and the Cuyamaca Training Area for jungle training. Another important training organization at San Diego was Troop Training Unit, Amphibious Training Command, Pacific Fleet. It provided amphibious training to the 4th and 5th MarDivs and 81st, 86th, 96th, and 97th InfDivs.

Not all Marines were part of the FMF. There were significant administrative, supply, and recruiting activities, the latter redesignated "procurement" in May 1943 after voluntary enlistment was eliminated in December 1942. All Marines were from that point conscripted, but most of the draftees had volunteered for the Marines Corps, as they were given a choice of service. Thousands of Marines served in Marine barracks and detachments to secure naval installations. In the States there were some 85 barracks and 30 detachments, and overseas there were over 30 barracks and five detachments. Over 22,000 Marines served aboard 500 ships in Marine ships' detachments during the war.

On Saipan, on the night of June 16/17, 1944, the Japanese battalion-sized 9th Tank Regiment launched a somewhat disorganized attack with 44 light and medium tanks on the 2d MarDiv's 1st Battalion, 6th Marines. Only six of the tanks survived the all-night battle, the largest Japanese tank attack experienced by the Marines to that date. Pictured here is a 57mm gun-armed Type 97 (1937) Chi-Ha medium tank, which comprised the bulk of the attacking tanks.

A new division

Pre-war plans foresaw the formation of a third Marine division, but not the eventual six. The 1st and 2d MarDivs had been organized in February 1941 from the existing 1st and 2d MarBdes. The 3d MarDiv was raised in September

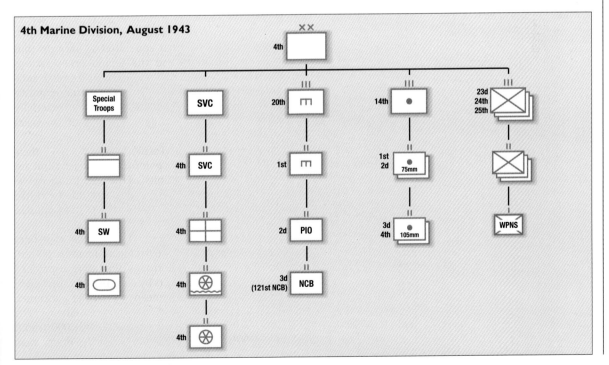

4th Marine Division, August 1943

Marine camps located on secured Pacific islands were austere, although efforts were made to provide a few amenities. Marines mostly lived under canvas in tent cities, but occasionally local materials and methods, and contracted labor were used, as demonstrated here by these 2d MarDiv officers' quarters on Goodenough Island off northeast New Guinea.

1942. As operations forged deeper into the vast Central Pacific area, a fourth division was raised.

The decision to organize the 4th MarDiv was made in early-1943. The 23d Marines, raised in July 1942 from a 9th Marines cadre at New River, NC and assigned to the 3d MarDiv, was reassigned to the as yet unactivated 4th MarDiv (being replaced by the 3d Marines) in February 1943. The 3d Battalion, 12th Marines [artillery] attached to the regiment was redesignated 3d Battalion, 14th Marines. The 25th Marines was activated in May at Camp Lejeune (formerly New River) by splitting the 23d Marines. The 24th Marines was organized at Camp Pendleton, CA in March from the 1st–3d Separate Battalions (Reinforced). The 14th Marines [artillery] was activated in June at Camp Pendleton and assigned to the Division in August. Its battalions had been raised with the infantry regiments. The 20th Marines [engineer] was organized from a 19th Marines cadre at Camp Lejeune in June. The 14th and 24th Marines at Camp Pendleton were identified as the West Coast Echelon. The 20th, 23d, and 25th Marines of the East Coast Echelon at Camp Lejeune relocated to Pendleton in July and August. The 4th MarDiv was activated there under the April 1943 T/O on August 16 under the acting command of BGen James L. Underhill. Two days later MajGen Harry Schmidt took command and Underhill became the assistant commander. The division undertook amphibious and tactical training until departing for the Central Pacific in January 1944 for attachment to VAC.

The 22d Marines was activated at Camp Linda Vista, CA in June 1942 with cadre provided by 6th and 9th Marines. As the first, separate, reinforced regiment organized after America's entry into the war, it was assigned to Defense Force, Samoan Group in July and attached to the 3d MarBde, FMF on Upolu, Western Samoa. It was detached from the 3d MarBde in May 1943, but remained assigned to the Defense Force until its departure in November. On arrival in Hawaii it was attached to Tactical Group 1, VAC, a provisional unit that served as the VAC Reserve in the Marshalls. The Group seized Eniwetok Atoll in February 1944, after which the 22d Marines moved to Guadalcanal.

In February 1944 the 4th Marines (Reinforced), lost on Corregidor in 1942, was reactivated at Tassafarougu, Guadalcanal from the 1st Raider Regiment. It had been planned to reactivate the 4th Marines from distinguished units. The 3d Battalion, 12th Marines (a second 3/12, different from the unit raised with the 23d Marines the year before) was redesignated Pack Howitzer Battalion, 4th Marines and other support units were assigned. This was made possible by the surplus of troops provided by the reorganization of the divisions. The 4th Marines was attached to Task Group A, IMAC. It was to have participated in the planned Kaveing, New Ireland operation attached to 3d MarDiv, but this was cancelled in March. The 3,727-man Group, under BGen Alfred H. Noble, 3d MarDiv Assistant Commander, secured unoccupied Emirau Island in the St Matthias Islands on March 20 in lieu of the Kaveing assault. The 106th Infantry, 27th InfDiv was attached for this operation. The Group returned to Guadalcanal in April.

The 22d and 4th Marines were assigned to the 1st Prov MarBde formed on April 19, 1944 on Guadalcanal. It would fight on Guam in July and August 1944 and in September would be expanded into the 6th MarDiv.

Fleet Marine Force, Pacific

In May 1944 a headquarters responsible for all FMF units in the Pacific was proposed: Amphibious Troops, Pacific. MajGen Holland Smith recommended a deployable Forward Headquarters, a General Headquarters to handle administrative functions at Pearl Harbor, Defense Troops to control

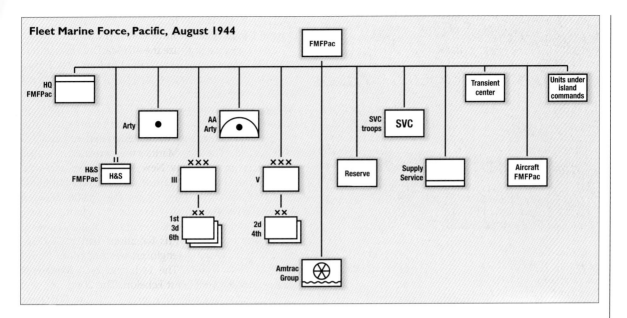

Fleet Marine Force, Pacific, August 1944

defense battalions and garrison units, Expeditionary Troops Artillery, a Service of Supply, the existing IMAC, the proposed IIMAC, and the Army's XIV Corps. Instead, IMAC was transferred from the Southwest Pacific Area to the Pacific Ocean Area joining VAC. VAC was given responsibility for the control of FMF administrative and logistical units in the Pacific. IMAC was redesignated IIIAC in April. While VAC handled administrative and supply functions, no single Marine headquarters controlled tactical operations. Since both IIIAC and VAC were committed to seizing the Marianas, a provisional headquarters was established under Holland Smith, also commanding VAC. Fleet Expeditionary Troops controlled both corps. Smith split the VAC staff into the Blue Staff for Fleet Expeditionary Troops and Red Staff for Northern Troops and Landing Force (VAC) to take Saipan and Tinian. IIIAC served as the Southern Troops and Landing Force to seize Guam.

While this summer campaign was in progress, on July 12, 1944 the decision was taken to formally establish Fleet Marine Forces, Pacific (FMFPac), headquartered at Camp Catlin, Oahu, TH under LtGen Holland Smith. Since Smith was in the Marianas, MajGen Harry Schmidt assumed temporary command. Smith formally assumed command on September 17 when he returned to Hawaii. The Blue Staff became the FMFPac staff and the Red Staff became the VAC staff. Marine Administrative Command, VAC became Administrative Command, FMFPac. Originally FMFPac was called Fleet Marine Forces, but was changed to "Force." As the Pacific Fleet's type command for FMF units, FMFPac consisted of a Headquarters and Service Battalion, Force Artillery, Force Anti-aircraft Artillery, Force Amphibian Tractor Group, Force Reserve, Force Service Troops, FMF Supply Service, and FMF Transient Center. IIIAC (1st, 3d MarDivs, 1st MarBde) and VAC (2d, 4th MarDivs) were assigned, as was Aircraft, FMFPac to control all Marine Aviation units.

A Marine on Saipan, with his pack configured in the field marching pack order, rushes for cover behind an embankment, passing a dud US Navy 6in. shell.

Unit organization

III Amphibious Corps' battle blaze, which would be worn on the left sleeve.

Marine organization maintained its triangular concept with units ranging from divisions to squads organized with three maneuver (infantry) subunits and a fire support unit. Special and service support units were organized in the triangular reinforcement concept possessing three subordinate units, allowing each to be attached in support of one of the parent unit's three maneuver subunits. As new types of weapons and equipment were fielded, new units were organized to accommodate them or existing units were internally reorganized to integrate them. The focus remained on a self-contained organization to accomplish the amphibious assault and its support.

Unit designation practices

Although much of the following background information appears in the first volume of this sequence, it is useful to repeat it here. Most Marine units were designated by number in their general order of activation according to type or function. Marine units were designated by function and not branch as was Army practice. While a table of organization (T/O) designated a unit as a "Marine infantry regiment," the Marines regarded "Infantry" as a functional designation rather than a branch or arm. In fact, while regiments were called infantry, artillery, or engineer by the T/O, those titles were not included in their designations. Marine regiments, regardless of type, were designated, for example, 24th Marines or 14th Marines without identifying their function. "Regiment" was not included in the designation.

There were exceptions to the sequential numbering of units upon activation, especially with regards to regiments, which were designated out of sequence of activation. The regiments are listed in the table to the left in order of activation, with their most recent activation date before or during World War II; the 1st–15th had been activated and deactivated earlier, some on more than one occasion. The 1st–9th Marines and 21st–29th Marines were infantry, the 10th–15th Marines were artillery, and the short-lived 16th–20th Marines were engineer regiments. In this book the artillery and engineer regiments are followed by their functional role in brackets for clarity, but it is emphasized that this identification was not part of the designation. By spring 1944 all regiments raised in World War II had been activated, with one last one being organized in October. Three (the 17th, the second 4th, and the 15th) were organized overseas. One, the 16th, never deployed overseas. The listed divisions were the regiments' final assignment—some were briefly assigned to other divisions, brigades, or were separate.

The six divisions were designated in their sequence of activation. They were called, for example, 4th Marine Division, never "4th Marine" so as not to confuse them

Marine regiments			
Regiment	Type	Activated	Division
4th (first)	Infantry	16 Apr 1914	separate*
5th	Infantry	1 Sep 34	1st
6th	Infantry	1 Sep 34	2d
8th	Infantry	1 Apr 40	2d
10th	Artillery	27 Dec 40	2d
7th	Infantry	1 Jan 41	1st
2d	Infantry	1 Feb 41	2d
1st	Infantry	1 Mar 41	1st
11th	Artillery	1 Mar 41	1st
9th	Infantry	12 Feb 42	3d
22d	Infantry	1 Jun 42	6th
3d	Infantry	16 Jun 42	3d
21st	Infantry	14 Jul 42	3d
23d	Infantry	22 Jul 42	4th
12th	Artillery	1 Sep 42	3d
18th	Engineer	8 Sep 42	2d
19th	Engineer	16 Sep 42	3d
17th	Engineer	12 Jan 43	1st
24th	Infantry	26 Mar 43	4th
25th	Infantry	1 May 43	4th
14th	Artillery	1 Jun 43	4th
20th	Engineer	15 Jun 43	4th
16th	Engineer	15 Dec 43	5th
13th	Artillery	10 Jan 44	5th
26th	Infantry	10 Jan 44	5th
27th	Infantry	10 Jan 44	5th
4th (second)	Infantry	1 Feb 44	6th
28th	Infantry	8 Feb 44	5th
29th	Infantry	1 May 44	6th
15th	Artillery	23 Oct 44	6th

Lost on Corregidor May 6, 1942.

with similarly numbered regiments such as the 4th Marines. Battalions in infantry and engineer regiments were designated 1st–3d while in artillery regiments they were the 1st–5th. In infantry regiments the companies were designated in sequence through the regiment: 1st Battalion—A to D; 2d Battalion—E to H; and 3d Battalion—I, and K to M (no company "J"). Companies D, H, and M were weapons companies, which were eliminated in the March 1944 reorganization. The rifle companies retained their original letter designations, with the sole exception of the 29th Marines, which had been organized after the change. Regimental weapons companies were designated as, for example, Weapons Company, 29th Marines. Battalions were simply shown as 1/5, pronounced "One/Five." Companies might be shown as D/6 and voiced using the phonetic alphabet as "Dog/Six" with no reference made to the battalion.

The number of battalions in artillery regiments varied from four to five at different times, but battalions always had three batteries. In four-battalion regiments the batteries were designated A–M and in five-battalion regiments as A–P (no battery "J"). By early-1944 they had only four battalions with most regiments giving up one battalion for conversion to an FMF 155mm howitzer battalion. The engineer regiments had three battalions: 1st—engineer; 2d—pioneer; and 3d—naval construction ("Seabees"), each with three companies designated A–I. When the engineer regiments were deactivated, the engineer and pioneer battalions remained assigned to their parent divisions and were redesignated with the division's number.

It is common practice to list Marine units from the highest echelon to lowest in numeric order, with units of the same echelon and numeric designation listed in alphabetical order by their functional designation.

1943–44 divisional organization

The Marine division underwent reorganization after the E-series T/O was approved on April 15, 1943. This mainly involved minor adjustments in personnel strength, additional weapons, deletion of the artillery regiment's special weapons battery, transfer of the special weapons battalion's 90mm AA

4th Marine Division's battle blaze.

V Amphibious Corps' battle blaze.

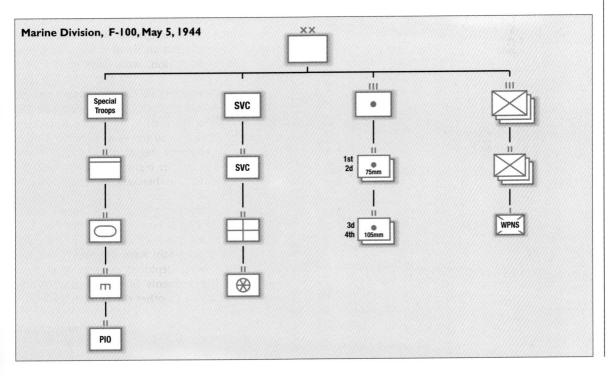

battery to defense battalions, and the reassignment of the parachute battalion to IMAC. Additional changes were made during the year. In the summer and fall of 1943 the scout company was reassigned from the tank battalion to the division HQ battalion. At the beginning of 1944 the amphibian tractor battalions began to operate under IMAC and VAC. Engineer regiments were no longer authorized from March 1944, but divisions retained them for some time. In November 1943 the 1st and 2d MarDivs had an authorized strength of 928 Marine officers (commissioned and warrant) and 17,192 enlisted with 133 Navy officers and 1,688 enlisted, making them the highest-strength divisions in the US armed forces.

The F-series division T/O was approved on May 5, 1944, although the infantry regiment T/O was approved in March. However, reorganization of infantry units began when HQMC provided draft T/Os to divisions in January. The deployed divisions were reorganized as follows:

Division	Location	Reorganized
1st	Pavavu Island	May–Jun 44
2d	Hawaii, TH	Feb–May 44
3d	Guadalcanal	May–Jun 44
4th	Maui, TH	Feb–Apr 44

This T/O saw streamlining of the infantry regiment, standardization of the artillery regiment with a reduction to four battalions, elimination of the engineer regiment (though they were retained well into 1944), the special weapons battalion was deleted, and the amphibian tractor battalion permanently assigned to FMF. This division had a paper strength of 843 Marine officers and 15,949 enlisted with 119 Navy officers and 955 enlisted; however, almost monthly changes of subordinate units' authorized strengths saw constant fluctuation, as demonstrated in the table below of authorized division strengths. The savings in personnel in each division were to be organized into separate infantry battalions, T/O E-5, bearing the division's number with an accompanying 75mm pack howitzer battery—totaling 1,066 troops. This

1944	Marine Corps		Navy	
Month	Officer	Enlisted	Officer	Enlisted
Jan	907	16,803	153	1,700*
Feb	860	16,632	161	1,783*
Mar	848	15,523	124	951
Apr	843	15,548	119	955
May	843	15,949	119	955
Jun	843	15,551	122	955
Jul	844	15,877	122	955
Aug	843	15,849	122	955
Sep	851	15,855	122	995
Oct	852	16,015	123	955
Nov	856	16,086	123	955
Dec	856	16,069	123	955
* Included the Seabee battalion.				

Marines root out by-passed Japanese sailors from the many dugouts and shelters on Roi-Namur. The half circle stenciled on the back of the Marines' jackets identified the 4th MarDiv. This same marking was also used on equipment and supplies.

was only accomplished in the 2d MarDiv with the activation of the 2d Separate Infantry Battalion (Reinforced) in April. It was redesignated 1st Battalion, 29th Marines on May 1, 1944. On average, the divisions were normally 1,000–2,000 men overstrength. Warrant officer (WO) strength is included in the officer strength; there were 90-plus warrant officers assigned to a division during this period. T/Os did not specify whether billets were held by 1st or 2d lieutenants, merely lieutenants.

It must be noted that unit strength figures given here are not absolute. Minor modifications to T/Os, as demonstrated previously, were frequent, resulting in slight changes. Additionally, the necessities of combat, introduction of new equipment, and frequent availability of additional personnel and weapons saw units going into combat organized and equipped somewhat differently than already obsolete T/Os allowed.

The infantry regiment

The infantry regiment changed little though the war, but the most significant changes were made in 1944 with the reallocation of crew-served weapons, introduction of new weapons, and refinements in subunit organization, all based on lessons learned in a year and a half of combat.

The 1943 infantry regiment possessed a regimental headquarters and service (HQ&S) company, three infantry battalions, and a weapons company. The HQ&S company consisted of company headquarters, scout and sniper platoon (optional), communication platoon, and regimental headquarters (with aid station); and intelligence, paymaster, and supply sections. The regimental weapons company had a headquarters, three platoons with four 37mm M3A1 anti-tank (AT) guns each, and a platoon with two self-propelled mount (SPM) M3 halftrack-mounted 75mm guns.

Infantry battalions had a HQ company, three rifle companies, and a weapons company. The HQ company had a company HQ and battalion HQ (with aid station), intelligence and supply sections, plus a communication platoon. The weapons company had a mortar platoon with four 81mm mortars and three machine-gun platoons each with four .30-cal. M1917A1 watercooled heavy machine guns (HMG).

Rifle companies had a headquarters, a weapons platoon, and three rifle platoons. The company HQ had two officers and 27 enlisted Marines. The 43-man rifle platoons had a headquarters with a lieutenant platoon leader, a platoon sergeant (his rank and position), platoon guide (sergeant), demolitions corporal, and three messengers. The three 12-man rifle squads had a squad leader (sergeant), assistant squad leader (corporal), two automatic riflemen, two assistants, and six riflemen armed with ten M1 rifles and two .30-cal. M1918A2 Browning automatic rifles (BAR). One rifleman had an M7 grenade launcher for his M1. The weapons platoon had a headquarters with a platoon leader (lieutenant), platoon sergeant, ammunition corporal, and a messenger; a 19-man machine-gun section of three squads (one .30-cal. M1919A4 aircooled light machine gun [LMG] each); and a 16-man mortar section with three squads (one 60mm M2 mortar each).

Infantry Regiment, Marine Division			
E-series T/O April 15, 1943	3,242	F-series T/O March 27, 1944	3,326
HQ&S Company	186	HQ&S Company	261
Infantry Battalion (x3)	953	Infantry Battalion (x3)	912
HQ Company	137	HQ Company	213
Company HQ	14	Company HQ	17
Battalion HQ	123	Battalion HQ	138
		81mm Mortar Platoon	58
Rifle Company (x3)	196	Rifle Company (x3)	247
Company HQ	28	Company HQ	53
Rifle Platoon (x3)	43	Rifle Platoon (x3)	46
Weapons Platoon	39	Machine Gun Platoon	56
Weapons Company	228	Deleted	
Company HQ	41		
Machine Gun Platoon (x3)	43		
81mm Mortar Platoon	58		
Regimental Weapons Company	197	Regimental Weapons Company	208
Company HQ	69	Company HQ	76
37mm AT Gun Platoon (x3)	34	37mm AT Gun Platoon (x3)	32
75mm SP Gun Platoon	26	75mm SP Gun Platoon	36

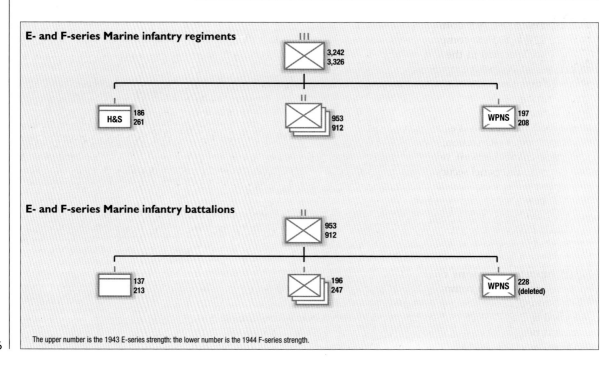

E- and F-series Marine infantry regiments

E- and F-series Marine infantry battalions

The upper number is the 1943 E-series strength: the lower number is the 1944 F-series strength.

The 1944 reorganization saw numerous changes in subunit strength and the reallocation of supporting weapons within the regiment. The most significant changes were the elimination of the battalion weapons companies (D, H, M), conversion of the rifle companies' weapons platoons to machine-gun platoons, and the elimination of the regimental HQ&S company's scout and sniper platoon. The removal of the weapons company HQs permitted additional personnel to be assigned to battalion and company headquarters, which increased their support capabilities.

Regimental HQ&S Company	Officers	Enlisted
Regimental HQ Section	14/5*	53/19 *
Intelligence Section		22
Paymaster Section	1/2 WO	9
Communication Platoon	1/1 WO	52
Platoon HQ	1/1 WO	3
Message Center & Messenger Section		12
Wire Section		19
Radio, Visual & Panel Section		24
Service Platoon	3/1 WO	67
Platoon HQ	1	17
Supply Section	1 WO	7
Munitions & Ordnance Section	1	3
Maintenance Section	1	16
Property Section		24
Commissary Section		6
Company HQ	1	18
* US Navy personnel		

The regimental HQ&S company
The regimental HQ&S company had a 72-man regimental HQ section. Although not specified in the T/O, it was internally organized into functional sections: R-1, 2, 3, and 4 staff sections; aid station, etc. All pay functions were centralized at regimental level to free the battalions of this task, and the clerks for the weapons company were assigned to the HQ&S company. The former supply section was expanded into a 71-man service platoon.

The HQ&S company was extremely lean on vehicles with only seven quarter-ton jeeps (three at HQ section, two at wire section, one at service platoon HQ, one at maintenance section), two more with TCS radios (one at HQ section; one at radio, visual and panel section), and five jeep ambulances in the HQ section. The property and commissary sections each had a one-ton cargo truck and the maintenance section a one-ton light repair truck. The one-ton 4 x 4 trucks were International M-2-4s. There were no crew-served weapons, only M1 rifles and M1 carbines plus a pool of 100 12-gauge M97/M12 riot shotguns for the infantry battalions.

The regimental weapons company
The regimental weapons company, commanded by a major, had three platoons, each with four 37mm M3A1 AT guns towed by one-ton trucks. Each gun section was crewed by five men. A lieutenant and ten enlisted Marines manned the HQ. A jeep and two one-ton ammunition trucks were assigned to the platoon HQ along with two 2.36in. M1A1 AT rocket launchers ("bazookas"). A fourth platoon

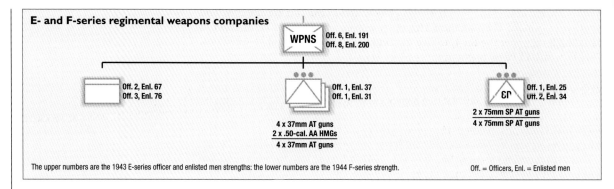

E- and F-series regimental weapons companies

WPNS — Off. 6, Enl. 191 / Off. 8, Enl. 200

Off. 2, Enl. 67 / Off. 3, Enl. 76

Off. 1, Enl. 37 / Off. 1, Enl. 31
4 x 37mm AT guns
2 x .50-cal. AA HMGs
4 x 37mm AT guns

Off. 1, Enl. 25 / Uff. 2, Enl. 34
2 x 75mm SP AT guns
4 x 75mm SP AT guns

The upper numbers are the 1943 E-series officer and enlisted men strengths: the lower numbers are the 1944 F-series strength.

Off. = Officers, Enl. = Enlisted men

had four 75mm M3 SPMs (each with a .30-cal. LMG, which could be ground mounted.) The two additional SPMs were gained from the deleted special weapons battalion. Its platoon HQ had two jeeps, two one-ton ammunition trucks, six bazookas, and a .30-cal. LMG. The platoon HQ had 14 enlisted Marines and, unusually, a captain CO and lieutenant XO. The weapons company HQ was organized into a two-officer 45-enlisted man HQ section, 20-man communication section, and a one-warrant officer eight-man maintenance section. The HQ had three jeeps (two with TCS radios), a one-ton cargo truck, and a one-ton light repair truck with a one-ton greasing trailer. It held a pool of ten .50-cal. HB-M2 HMGs, six on AA mounts and four for vehicle or ground mounting, plus six .30-cal. LMGs, for which three-man crews were provided for regimental HQ security. The company HQ section had 17 bazookas while the maintenance section had four. The pool of .50-cal. HMGs and bazookas could be issued to other elements of the regiment, and were a source for the rifle platoons.

Infantry battalion HQ company

The infantry battalion's HQ company was organized into three elements: battalion HQ, 81mm mortar platoon, and company HQ. The 79-man HQ section was usually subdivided into Bn-1, 2, 3, and 4 staff sections, clerical section, etc., plus the aid station, which contained the bulk of the section's personnel (44 Navy medical staff with five Marine ambulance drivers.) The communication platoon

Infantry Battalion HQ Company	Officers	Enlisted
Battalion HQ Section	9/2*	28/42*
Intelligence Section		12
Supply Section	I WO	6
Communication Platoon	I	39
Platoon HQ	I	2
Message Center & Messenger Section		8
Wire Section		14
Radio, Visual & Panel Section		15
81mm Mortar Platoon	2	56
Platoon HQ	2	6
Mortar Section (x2)		25
Section HQ		11
Mortar Squad (x2)		7
Company HQ	I	17
* US Navy personnel		

plus intelligence and supply sections, separate from but working for the Bn-2 and Bn-4, were part of the battalion HQ. All company clerks were centralized at battalion level under the Bn-1, to free the companies of administrative functions. This system had been previously tested by the 1st and 2d MarDivs. Company cobblers could be consolidated at battalion level to operate a shoe and textile repair section. The former battalion weapons company's 58-man mortar platoon with four 81mm M1 mortars was reassigned to the HQ company. It was organized to operate in two two-squad sections. It maintained four 60mm mortars as alternative weapons. Pooled in the battalion supply section were 27 M1A1 flamethrowers and 27 No. 5 demolition kits—one of each per rifle squad.

The battalion HQ section had two jeeps, the wire section had one, and the radio, visual and panel section had one with a TCS radio. The two mortar section headquarters each had a jeep with a quarter-ton trailer and otherwise relied on two MC-1942 handcarts per squad to haul the mortar and ammunition.

The rifle company

Each rifle company had a HQ, three rifle platoons, and a machine-gun platoon. The former company weapons platoon was converted to machine guns only

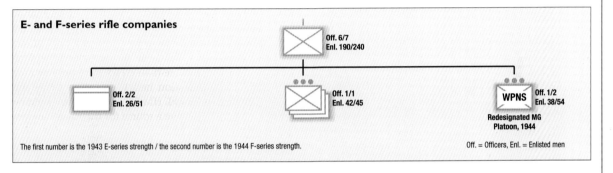

E- and F-series rifle companies

Off. 6/7
Enl. 190/240

Off. 2/2
Enl. 26/51

Off. 1/1
Enl. 42/45

WPNS
Off. 1/2
Enl. 38/54

Redesignated MG
Platoon, 1944

The first number is the 1943 E-series strength / the second number is the 1944 F-series strength.

Off. = Officers, Enl. = Enlisted men

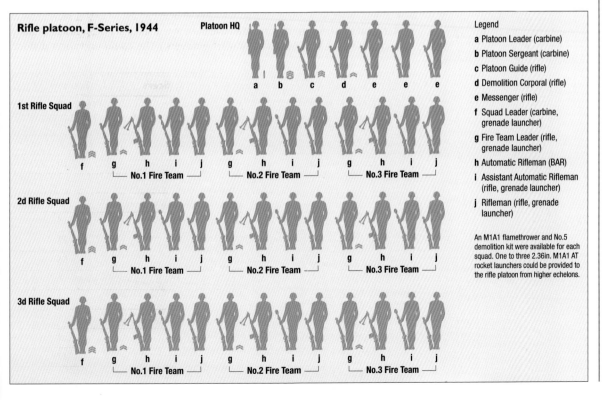

Rifle platoon, F-Series, 1944

Platoon HQ

a   b   c   d   e   e   e

1st Rifle Squad

f   g   h   i   j   g   h   i   j   g   h   i   j
    └─ No.1 Fire Team ─┘   └─ No.2 Fire Team ─┘   └─ No.3 Fire Team ─┘

2d Rifle Squad

f   g   h   i   j   g   h   i   j   g   h   i   j
    └─ No.1 Fire Team ─┘   └─ No.2 Fire Team ─┘   └─ No.3 Fire Team ─┘

3d Rifle Squad

f   g   h   i   j   g   h   i   j   g   h   i   j
    └─ No.1 Fire Team ─┘   └─ No.2 Fire Team ─┘   └─ No.3 Fire Team ─┘

Legend

a Platoon Leader (carbine)
b Platoon Sergeant (carbine)
c Platoon Guide (rifle)
d Demolition Corporal (rifle)
e Messenger (rifle)
f Squad Leader (carbine, grenade launcher)
g Fire Team Leader (rifle, grenade launcher)
h Automatic Rifleman (BAR)
i Assistant Automatic Rifleman (rifle, grenade launcher)
j Rifleman (rifle, grenade launcher)

An M1A1 flamethrower and No.5 demolition kit were available for each squad. One to three 2.36in. M1A1 AT rocket launchers could be provided to the rifle platoon from higher echelons.

Engineer Assault Team (attached to each rifle platoon), 1st Battalion, 18th Marines, Tarawa, November 1943

Legend

a Team Leader (carbine)
b Flamethrower Operator (flamethrower, pistol)
c Assistant Flamethrower Operator (shotgun)
d Demolition Man (rifle)

The handcart carried:

50 x 0.5 lb TNT charges	2 x spare hydrogen tanks	100ft of detonating cord
50 x 2.25 lb C-2 charges	2 x AN-M14 incendiary grenades	50ft of time safety fuse
2 x M1 Bangalore torpedoes	6 x Mk III A1 demolition grenades	
2 x 5-gal cans of flame fuel	100 x non-electric blasting caps	

with six .30-cal. M1919A4 LMGs. The two-officer, 31-enlisted company HQ section had six reserve .30-cal. M1917A1 HMGs, which could be substituted for the LMGs. The one-officer, 19-enlisted mortar section, previously part of the weapons platoon, was reassigned to the company HQ with three 60mm M2 mortars. It now rated a lieutenant leader and a section sergeant in its headquarters and had three six-man squads. There were three bazookas in the company HQ to be allocated as necessary. The HQ section had a jeep with a quarter-ton trailer.

The rifle platoon had a seven-man headquarters, organized as the 1943 T/O, and three 13-man rifle squads organized under a new concept. It had a squad leader (M1 carbine) and three four-man fire teams designated No. 1–3, each with a team leader (corporal, M1 rifle, M7 grenade launcher), rifleman (M1 rifle, M7 grenade launcher), Browning automatic rifleman (M1918A2 BAR), and an assistant automatic rifleman (M1 rifle, M7 launcher). Initially the assistant BAR-men were armed with carbines and M8 grenade launchers, but these were soon replaced by more effective rifles.

This organization gave the squad three fire and maneuver elements, each led by a designated leader. Its concept went back to the Banana Wars in the late-1920s. The then 1stLt Merritt Edson, 5th Marines (later to command the 1st Raider Battalion) divided rifle squads into three- and four-man "fighting groups," each with a BAR, Lewis LMG, or Thompson submachine gun (SMG). It proved to be an effective technique in jungle fighting. Maj Edson, now in the 4th Marines in China, further developed the concept into "fighting teams" in the 1930s. The 1st and 2d Raider battalions unofficially used this organization when raised in 1941 as "fire groups" with three men each—three per squad. The 4th Marines, organized from the raider battalions, continued to use the fire-team concept and formal testing was conducted by Training Battalion, Marine Corps schools and L/3/24 Marines in the States. It was combat tested on Eniwetok in February 1944 by the 22d Marines. That month, rifle companies were directed to begin reorganizing into fire teams. It would not be until June that all units were reorganized. Fire-team leaders gave squad leaders an additional degree of control, allowing small units to continue their missions even when communications were lost and under heavy fire. It provided a triangular organization with a leader at every level controlling three maneuver elements; in the case of the fire-team leader his three elements were individual Marines. A system of voice and arm and hand signals was developed, allowing squad leaders to shift teams and individuals quickly into different formations, to confront any tactical situation. There was a key difference in that the fire-team leaders led by example, whereas other leaders gave commands. They followed the squad leader's orders and carried them out, and what they did, their men did.

The artillery regiment

The 1943 artillery regiment standardized the allocation to artillery battalions of three 75mm M1A1 pack howitzer and two 105mm M2A1 howitzer battalions. This structure allocated one 75mm battalion to each infantry regiment and provided two 105mm battalions for general support.

Battalion HQ&S batteries consisted of a battalion HQ, battery headquarters and maintenance sections, and communication, operations, and service platoons. Artillery batteries were organized into three elements. The battery HQ had headquarters, local security, and maintenance sections. The battery detail had headquarters, forward observer, and communication sections. The firing battery had a headquarters, an ammunition and four howitzer sections, each with one piece regardless of caliber.

Artillery Regiment, Marine Division			
E-series T/O April 15, 1943	3,207	F-series T/O May 5, 1944	2,639
HQ&S Battery	204	HQ&S Battery	229
75mm Artillery Battalion (x3)	605	75mm Artillery Battalion (x2)	603
HQ&S Battery	152	HQ&S Battery	159
75mm Howitzer Battery (x3)	151	75mm Howitzer Battery (x3)	148
105mm Artillery Battalion (x2)	594	105mm Howitzer Battalion (x2)	602
HQ&S Battery	150	HQ&S Battery	161
105mm Artillery Battery (x3)	148	105mm Howitzer Battery (x3)	147

The 1944 reorganization saw the reassignment of one of the 75mm battalions to FMF for conversion to 155mm howitzer. This provided corps-level artillery battalions without the need to raise new battalions. The new organization envisaged the two remaining 75mm battalions would be attached to the two assault regiments in direct support, the reserve regiment would be supported by one of the 105mm battalions, and the other 105mm battalion would be in general support. Both 105mm battalions could provide general support though.

The removal of one 75mm battalion often resulted in the redesignation of another battalion in order to maintain numeric sequence within the regiment. The battalions armed with 75mm and 105mm howitzers bore different designations in some divisions. In most cases the 1st and 2d battalions were armed with the 75mm and the 3d and 4th with the 105mm.

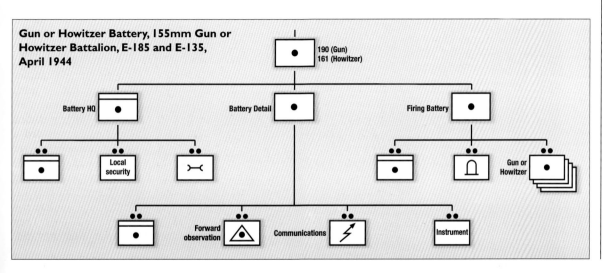

Gun or Howitzer Battery, 155mm Gun or Howitzer Battalion, E-185 and E-135, April 1944

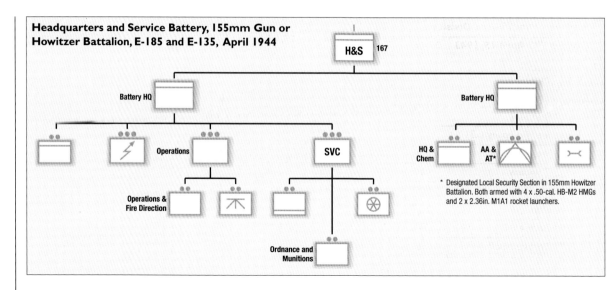

Headquarters and Service Battery, 155mm Gun or Howitzer Battalion, E-185 and E-135, April 1944

H&S 167

Battery HQ

Operations

Operations & Fire Direction

SVC

Ordnance and Munitions

Battery HQ

HQ & Chem

AA & AT*

* Designated Local Security Section in 155mm Howitzer Battalion. Both armed with 4 x .50-cal. HB-M2 HMGs and 2 x 2.36in. M1A1 rocket launchers.

Artillery regiment reorganization, 1944	
10th Marines, 2d MarDiv	5/10 redesignated 2d 155mm Howitzer Battalion, 16 Apr 44
11th Marines, 1st MarDiv	3/11 redesignated 3d 155mm Howitzer Battalion, 7 May 44
	5/11 redesignated 3/11, 7 May 44
12th Marines, 3d MarDiv	3/12 redesignated Pack Howitzer Battalion, 4th Marines, 30 Mar 44
	5/12 redesignated 3/12, 30 Mar 44
14th Marines, 4th MarDiv	5/14 redesignated 4th 105mm Howitzer Battalion, 1 Mar 44
	Converted to 155mm, 23 Nov 44

Engineer regiments

Engineer regiments were organized between September 1942 and December 1943 from the existing divisional engineer and pioneer battalions plus a naval construction battalion (NCB, or Seabee). The new regiment would control the division's shore party. Prior to the activation of the regiments the first two battalions carried the division's number. Under the regiment the engineer battalion became the 1st, pioneer battalion the 2d, and the NCB the 3d, though it was often known by its original two-digit Navy designation.

The engineer battalion's companies were intended for habitual attachment to infantry regiments, explaining the small HQ company, with most being commanded by majors (the division staff engineer officer was a lieutenant-colonel). The three engineer companies had a headquarters, an assault platoon, and an engineer platoon, sometimes called a construction platoon. The platoons were organized into three sections for attachment to infantry battalions. Some battalions, such as the 2d MarDiv's at Tarawa, organized into a 77–84-man construction platoon and three 56–60-man assault platoons. Its three 19-man squads had a squad leader and three six-man assault teams—one per rifle platoon (see the diagram on page 20). The pioneer battalions were essentially stevedore units intended to unload landing craft, organize dumps, and move supplies forward, but could perform construction tasks in support of the beach party. The three pioneer companies had a headquarters and three platoons. The Seabee battalion assisted the beach party, and built support facilities, airstrips, and roads in the division rear. Its three companies had a headquarters and six assorted platoons: maintenance and operations; two construction; road blasting and excavation; waterfront; and tanks, steel, and pipes.

Engineer units, Marine Division			
E-series T/O April 15, 1943	2,517	F-series Engineer and Pioneer battalions	
HQ&S Company	290	*Deleted*	
Engineer Battalion	645	Engineer Battalion	904
HQ Company	60	HQ Company	307
Engineer Company (x3)	195	Engineer Company (x3)	199
Pioneer Battalion	744	Pioneer Battalion	745
HQ Company	120	HQ Company	127
Pioneer Company (x3)	208	Pioneer Company (x3)	206
NC Battalion	838	*Reassigned to Navy*	
HQ Company	157		
NC Company (x3)	227		

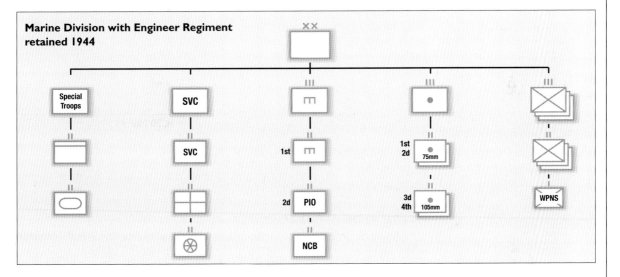

Marine Division with Engineer Regiment retained 1944

A criticism of the engineer regiment was that the Seabee battalion was unavailable for other assignments when the division was rebuilding after an operation. The Navy reasoned that Seabee battalions should be withdrawn and tasked with new assignments; they suffered few casualties during most operations. The Navy would attach an uncommitted Seabee battalion from its pool of over 100 when a division was assigned a combat mission. Regular Seabee battalions had four companies rather than three as the divisional battalions—totaling 1,105 men.

The engineer regiments were ordered deactivated in March 1944 with the uncommitted 5th MarDiv's 16th Marines standing down in May. The deactivation of the overseas divisions' regiments was delayed though. The 2d, 3d, and 4th MarDivs were preparing to assault the Marianas and the engineer regiments' training, embarkation plans, and integration into the maneuver scheme were already developed. The Seabees remained attached, but not assigned. The deactivation of the 18th, 19th, and 20th Marines was delayed until August and September, after the operations were completed. The 1944 engineer battalion's HQ company went from 60 men to over 300, absorbing many of the service and specialist troops of the former regimental HQ&S company. The companies were reorganized into three common engineer platoons to allow one to be attached to each infantry battalion.

Special troops

The reassignment of the divisional parachute battalions to IMAC in March 1943, followed by the inactivation of the special weapons battalion with the introduction of the May 1944 T/O led to the demise of the special troops as an entity. The remaining HQ and tank battalions simply became divisional units along with the engineer and pioneer battalions. The special weapons battalions' SPM 75mm gun-armed half-tracks were reassigned to the regimental weapons companies and the 37mm AT guns deleted. The 40mm AA battery was reassigned to the new AAA battalions. The tank battalion's scout company (Company D) had been reassigned to the HQ battalion in the summer and fall of 1943. This assignment was formerly reflected in the 1944 T/O. Its organization is discussed in the chapter on intelligence (see pp 47–48).

The tank companies

In 1944 tank companies underwent a major reorganization that proved to be less than desirable. The 1943 light-tank company had three five-tank platoons with three more tanks in the headquarters equipped with M3A3, M5, or M5A1 tanks. The 37mm gun-armed tanks had difficulties in dense jungle terrain, mud, and on broken ground. The 37mm proved inadequate against pillboxes. The 1st Corps Tank Battalion (Medium), intended to provide M4A2 Sherman tank companies for attachment to divisions, was deactivated on February 15, 1944 on New Caledonia. Its tanks were transferred to divisional battalions as they phased in medium tanks: companies A and B went to 3d MarDiv, Company C went to 2d MarDiv, and Company D (without tanks) went to 4th MarDiv. It was organized as Company D (Flamethrower), 4th Tank Battalion. The 1st Light Tank Battalion had converted its Company A to M4A1s prior to the New Britain landing, exchanging its M2A4s in Australia. The other two companies received M5A1s from Army stocks. The battalions were not completely equipped with Shermans and some were committed to combat with one or two medium companies and the rest light. Along with the Shermans each company received an M32B2 tank recovery vehicle, built on an M4A2 tank chassis.

The five-tank platoons proved to be difficult to control in jungles. The 1944 F-80 T/O saw the new medium companies reorganized into four three-tank platoons with three in the headquarters, one of which was fitted with a dozer blade. This provided an additional platoon to allow more flexible attachment to infantry battalions and made control easier. The problem was that by the time this structure was adopted the fighting had shifted to smaller, moderately vegetated islands. The small platoons lost their effectiveness if even one tank was knocked out or suffered a mechanical failure. Two of the small platoons often had to be attached to a battalion to provide effective support. A return to

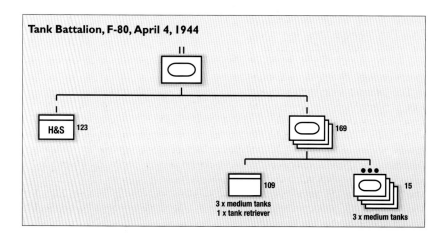

Tank Battalion, F-80, April 4, 1944

H&S 123

169

109
3 x medium tanks
1 x tank retriever

15
3 x medium tanks

the three five-tank platoon was desired, but was not approved until after the war. On Saipan and Tinian the 2d and 4th Tank Battalions fielded a provisional Company D with three platoons, each with six M3A1 flame-tanks and two M5A1 gun-tanks for support.

Special Troops, Marine Division			
E-series T/O April 15, 1943	2,536	F-series T/O May 5, 1944	1,891
Division HQ	211	Division HQ	257
HQ Battalion	861	HQ Battalion	1,004
HQ Company	420	HQ Company	483
Signal Company	340	Signal Company	292
MP Company	101	MP Company	102
		Reconnaissance Company	127
Light Tank Battalion	707	Tank Battalion	630
HQ&S Company	85	HQ&S Company	123
Light Tank Company (x3)	161	Tank Company (x3)	169
Scout Company	139	Reassigned to HQ Battalion	
Special Weapons Battalion	757	Deleted	
HQ&S Battery	102	Deleted	
AT Battery (x3)	116	Deleted, some assets to infantry regts	
40mm AA Gun Battery	307	Reassigned to FMF AAA battalions	

Service troops

The service troops remained a robust organization with the capacity to support a full division. The service battalion's service and supply company, commanded by a major, provided a full range of logistical support. It had four 100-man-plus service platoons with service and supply, salvage, chemical service, bakery, commissary, post exchange, bath, and graves registration sections. The four-platoon ordnance company provided weapons and vehicle maintenance support. Three of the four three-platoon "Motor-T" companies were habitually attached to infantry regiments. Three of the medical battalion's companies were attached to infantry regiments augmenting the regimental aid stations with the other two serving as clearing companies and supporting other units. There were three platoons per company.

The amphibian tractor battalions were attached to FMF in January 1944 and deleted from the May 1944 T/O. This allowed these important units to be pooled for attachment to divisions as required. They had evolved from carrying supplies across reefs and inland to delivering assault troops under fire.

The Marine Corps' first attempt at a rocket unit was a minimal effort in the form of the 1st Corps Experimental Rocket Platoon in June 1943. It was armed with 4.5in. T27E1 single-tube rocket launchers and 2.36in. M1 bazookas. Through 1944 the 1st–5th Rocket Detachments (Provisional) were formed for attachment to divisions: 1st—4th MarDiv; 2d—2d MarDiv; 3d—5th MarDiv; 4th—1st MarDiv; 5th—6th MarDiv. (3d MarDiv did not receive the 6th until July 1945.) A detachment had three officers and 53 enlisted Marines

Marine infantry units desperately lacked trucks, and relied heavily on divisional and corps motor transport battalions. Here an International 2.5-ton M-3-L4 six-wheel-drive cargo truck struggles through the New Britain mud. Most Marine trucks were painted dark green, known simply as Marine Corps Green, and had yellow registration numbers.

organized into a small headquarters and two sections, each with six one-ton trucks mounting three gravity-fed 4.5in. Mk 7 launcher racks. The "Buck Rogers Men," as they were known after the science fiction comic book hero, provided an excellent area fire capability for counterbattery missions.

Service Troops, Marine Division				
E-series T/O April 15, 1943	**2,200**	**F-series T/O May 5, 1944**		**1,886**
Amphibian Tractor Battalion	486	*Transferred to FMF Jan 44*		
HQ&S Company	81	*deleted from T/O May 44*		
Amphibian Tractor Coy (x3)	135			
Medical Battalion	526	Medical Battalion		599
HQ&S Company	21	HQ&S Company		89
Medical Company (x5)	101	Medical Company (x5)		102
Motor Transport Battalion	527	Motor Transport Battalion		539
HQ&S Company	188	HQ&S Company		194
Transport Company (x3)	113	Transport Company (x3)		115
Service Battalion	661	Service Battalion		748
HQ Company	62	HQ Company		68
Service and Supply Company	455	Service and Supply Company		502
Ordnance Company	144	Ordnance Company		178

Separate infantry regiment organization

The Marine Corps continued to organize separate infantry regiments. They generally operated as part of a brigade or tactical group. All were eventually rolled into divisions. Changes in the separate regiment T/Os followed those of the divisional regiments, but with assigned units normally organic to the parent division. The 4,823-man 1944 separate regiment T/O eliminated the amphibian tractor, anti-tank, and Seabee companies and the 40mm AA platoon. From 1944 the regimental tank companies were equipped with M4A2s. Three regiments served under these T/Os: the 22d, raised in June 1942; the 4th, organized in February 1944; and the 29th, activated in May 1944. The 4th, and 22d would see combat as separate regiments and would fight together as part of the 1st Prov MarBde. All three regiments were consolidated into the 6th MarDiv in September 1944. The separate regiments' reinforcing units were usually identified by the regimental number, e.g. Tank Company, 4th Marines.

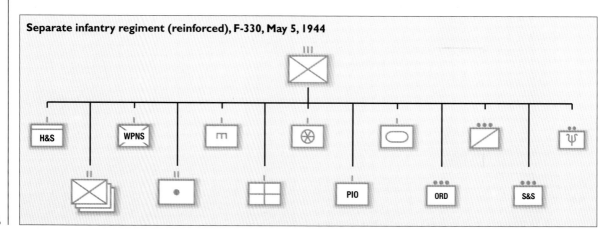

Separate infantry regiment (reinforced), F-330, May 5, 1944

Separate Infantry Regiment (Reinforced) F-330, May 5, 1944	4,823
HQ&S Company, Infantry Regiment	261
Infantry Battalion (x3)	918
HQ Company	213
Rifle Company (x3)	235
Regimental Weapons Company	203
75mm Artillery Battalion	603
HQ&S Battery	159
75mm Pack Howitzer Battery (x3)	148
Engineer Company	199
Medical Company	102
Motor Transport Company	115
Pioneer Company	206
Tank Company	169
Ordnance Platoon	35
Reconnaissance Platoon	33
Service and Supply Platoon	114
Band Section	29

Splitting the defense battalions

Even in 1942 the need for the defense battalions, at least in their current structure, was being questioned as Japanese offensive capabilities deteriorated. Japan retained the capability of conducting air attacks on US forces in the forward areas. The Japanese had attempted few counterlandings on American beachheads, an original major concern. After Guadalcanal there were virtually no attempts by Japanese surface ships to attack American beachheads. The defense battalions' 155mm coast defense guns were now directed inland to attack Japanese ground forces. By March 1944 there were 20 defense battalions (1st–18th, 51st, 52d). The battalions' AA guns, while still defending against air attack, were also used to engage ground targets and were well suited to defending against Japanese barges attempting rare counterlandings and raids. The Marines wished to reorganize the battalions while the Navy wanted nine more to secure advanced bases. The Marine Corps, with its manpower

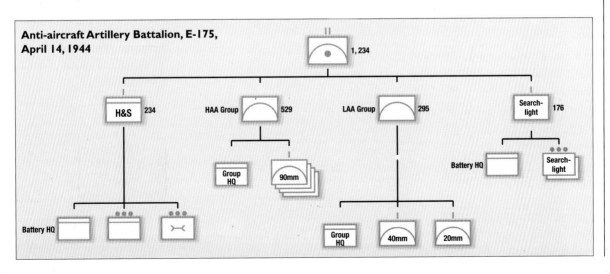

Anti-aircraft Artillery Battalion, E-175, April 14, 1944 — 1,234; H&S 234; HAA Group 529; LAA Group 295; Search-light 176

From December 1943 the training of defense battalion personnel was conducted in the Artillery Battalion, Training Center, FMF, Camp Lejeune, North Carolina. Here crewmen practice on a 5in. Mk 15 Model 0 seacoast defense gun.

resources stretched, did not want to be tied down any more than necessary garrisoning islands. It wanted units capable of supporting offensive operations. The Army would provide additional AAA battalions to aid in garrisoning island bases.

In March 1944 the 3d, 4th, 9th, 11th, 12th, and 14th defense battalions, scattered through the Solomons, were assigned to Corps Defense Troops, IMAC. The previous month the 1st, 2d, 5th, 7th, 10th, and 15th–17th defense battalions had been assigned to Corps Defense Troops, VAC garrisoning the Ellices, Gilberts, and Marshalls. These commands were disbanded in April and the battalions began to be reorganized to function more effectively in the two different roles: air defense and indirect fire support. Most defense battalions were split and reorganized into FMF AAA and 155mm gun battalions.

Most of the defense battalions were reorganized and redesignated AAA battalions between April and September. The first six 1,210-man battalions reorganized in April were initially redesignated AA battalions. They were redesignated AAA in June, as were all subsequent battalions. There were no differences between the two battalions. Only the 6th, 51st, and 52d defense battalions remained designated as such into 1945. The latter two were manned by African-American enlisted Marines. The AAA battalions were still commanded by full colonels.

Anti-aircraft Artillery Battalion, E-174, April 14, 1944	1,210
HQ&S Battery	200
HQ Platoon	117
Maintenance Platoon	51
Battery HQ	32
Searchlight Battery	176
Heavy AAA Group	539
Group HQ	55
90mm AA Battery (x4)	121
Light AAA Group	295
Group HQ	37
40mm AA Battery	177
20mm AA Battery	81

The searchlight battery had twelve 60in. Sperry lights and there were four SCR-270D radar sets in the HQ&S battery. The four 90mm batteries each had four 90mm M1A1 AA guns, an SCR-584 fire-control radar plus a machine-gun section with four .50-cal. M2 watercooled AA HMGs for close-in air defense. Each of a battery's four 90mm gun sections also had two .30-cal. M1917A1 HMGs for beach defense, in case the 90mm's had already been knocked out. The two light batteries had either twelve 40mm M1 or twelve 20mm twin Mk 4 AA guns. Each 40mm gun section possessed a .50-cal. HB-M2 aircooled HMG.

The reorganization of the defense battalions led to the reassignment of their seacoast artillery groups to new FMF 155mm artillery battalions (gun) in the spring of 1944. The 10th had been formed from the existing 1st 155mm Artillery Battalion (Provisional) in March while the 2d 155mm Artillery Battalion (Provisional) became the 7th. The 8th was organized from the 4th and 8th Defense Battalions' seacoast artillery groups, the 9th from the 12th Defense Battalion's group, and the 11th and 12th from the 2d, 5th, 7th, and 16th defense battalions. In late-June all battalions were redesignated 155mm gun battalions. These 738-man battalions had a 167-man HQ&S battery and three 190-man gun batteries, each with four 155mm M1A1 "Long Tom" guns. These battalions possessed Mk XVI and SO-7M radars to allow them to be used for coast defense, a mission they were never called on to perform. Instead the 7th–9th battalions were attached to IIIAC and the 10th–12th to VAC for which they provided counterbattery and long-range fire. In the fall of 1944 the 1st–3d Seacoast Artillery battalions were formed on Maui, TH from the seacoast artillery groups of the 9th, 14th, and 15th Defense Battalions and assigned to the 1st Seacoast Artillery Group (Provisional).

At the same time, 650-man FMF 155mm artillery battalions (howitzer) were formed, mainly by rearming battalions contributed by divisions as previously discussed. In June they were redesignated 155mm howitzer battalions. The 5th Battalion was formed by converting the 12th 155mm Gun Battalion in July. A new 12th Battalion was organized almost immediately. They had a 167-man HQ&S battery and three 161-man howitzer batteries, each with four 155mm M1A1 howitzers. The 1st, 3d, and 6th battalions were attached to IIIAC and the 2d, 4th, and 5th to VAC.

Amphibian units

The 1st–4th Amphibian Tractor Battalions, originally organic to divisions, were reassigned to corps troops in May 1944 and to FMFPac in September, but had been detached from the divisions since January to support IMAC and VAC. Those 486-man battalions had been organized with their parent divisions, but the subsequent battalions were all raised at Camp Pendleton, home of the amtracs, with the exception of the provisional 6th formed in the Russells. The 10th was activated in December 1943 followed by the 5th in February 1944, the 8th and 9th in May, the 11th in June, and the 6th in July. (No 7th was raised.) Divisional battalions originally had three companies, but as non-divisional battalions they could have up to five companies. A company possessed three platoons of nine amtracs each plus three in the company HQ. Ten more were in the HQ&S company. In practice the number could be more or less. In some instances companies within the same battalion were equipped with different models, namely a mix of LVT(2)s and LVT(4)s. Amtracs were temperamental and maintenance intensive. A battalion was issued eight railroad boxcars of spare parts.

The 1st Armored Amphibian Tractor Battalion was activated in August 1943, equipped with LVT(A)1s (armed with an M3 light tank 37mm gun turret, one .50-cal., three or four .30-cal.), and first employed at Roi-Namur in January 1944 by VAC. That same month the 2d was organized to serve with VAC. IIIAC formed the provisional 3d Battalion in July in the Russells. It initially had one

New amtracs
The original LVT(1) Alligator was last used at New Britain, before being replaced in early-1944. The improved LVT(2) Water Buffalo was first used at Tarawa in November 1943 and became the mainstay amtrac until mid-1944. Both the LVT(1) and (2) lacked rear ramps. They carried 20 troops or 4,500 lbs of cargo and 24 troops or 6,500 lbs respectively. They were armed with a .50-cal. and up to three .30-cal. machine guns. The LVT(4) first saw service at Saipan in July 1944 and replaced the LVT(2), although it remained in limited use to the end of the war. The LVT(3) was not fielded until 1945 due to production delays. The LVT(4) had a rear ramp, which greatly improved its capabilities. It could carry 24 troops or 8,000 lbs of cargo to include a 105mm howitzer or jeep, the first amtrac that could do so. There were 18,616 amtracs of all marks built during the war with some provided to the Allies. Of those used by the US, the Army employed 55 percent, the Navy 5 percent, while the Marines procured the remaining 40 percent in the following quantities:

LVT(1)	540	LVT(4)	1,765
LVT(2)	1,355	LVT(A)1	182
LVT(3)	2,962	LVT(A)4	533

company of LVT(A)1s and two of LVT(A)4s. In mid-1944 the LVT(A)1s began to be replaced by LVT(A)4s (armed with an M8 self-propelled 75mm howitzer turret, one .50-cal., and one .30-cal.). An 852-man battalion had an HQ&S company and four companies, each with three platoons of six armored amtracs. Twelve cargo amtracs were distributed through the battalion.

The amphibian truck companies equipped with the 2.5-ton DUKW-353 or "Duck" were also important amphibian transport units. Adopted by the Army in 1943, it would be almost a year before the 1st and 2d Marine Amphibian Truck Companies at Camp Elliott were organized (this took place at the end of 1943.) They were first used at Saipan and proved so successful that VAC formed the provisional 3d–6th companies in October and December 1944. A company's 40–50 Ducks were mainly used to haul artillery and their ammunition ashore. The howitzers were driven across the reefs, over the beach, and directly to their firing positions where they were off-loaded by an A-frame hoist. No prime mover was needed until landed from landing craft in later waves. The Ducks then evacuated wounded and returned with more ammunition, delivering it directly to the batteries.

Amphibious corps organization

I Marine Amphibious Corps was organized on October 1, 1942 at San Diego using the staff of Amphibious Corps, Pacific Fleet (PhibCorpsPacFlt). It soon moved to Hawaii to serve as an administrative headquarters for Marine units in the Pacific. It was quickly realized that a headquarters was required to plan and coordinate combat operations. IMAC went on to plan and control operations in the Solomons. Commanded by MajGen Roy S. Geiger since November 1943 and headquartered on Guadalcanal, it oversaw the occupation of the Green Islands between the Solomons and the Bismarcks in February 1944. It was planned for IMAC to assault Kaveing, New Ireland with the 3d MarDiv and 40th InfDiv, but this was cancelled in March. Having previously served under the Southwest Pacific Area, IMAC was transferred to Pacific Ocean Area command on March 25, 1944. Still on Guadalcanal, IMAC was redesignated IIIAC on April 15, 1944. At the same time Amphibious Force, South Pacific was redesignated Third Amphibious Force, part of Third Fleet. The 1st and 3d MarDivs and 3d New Zealand Division were under IMAC.

As the former PhibCorpsPacFlt staff became the IMAC staff, Amphibious Training Staff, FMF under MajGen Holland M. Smith arrived from the East Coast and took over command of PhibCorpsPacFlt on October 1, 1942. PhibCorpsPacFlt continued training Marine and Army units for amphibious operations. On August 25, 1943 it was redesignated V Amphibious Corps (VAC) to support the Navy's Fifth Amphibious Force, itself commissioned on August 15 as part of Fifth Fleet. VAC moved to Hawaii the next month and planned combat operations that would commence in the Gilberts in November 1943 and continue in the Marshalls in January 1944. Smith was promoted to lieutenant general on March

In the table below, the dates to the right of the IMAC units refer to their activation. These were redesignated IIIAC units on April 15, 1944. The dates to the right of the IIIAC units refer to their deactiviation.

I Marine Amphibious Corps, FMF		III Amphibious Corps, FMFPac	
1st Corps HQ&S Battalion	Sep 43	IIIAC HQ&S Battalion	Jun 46
1st Corps Medical Battalion	Dec 42	IIIAC Medical Battalion	Mar 46
1st Corps MT Battalion	Oct 42	IIIAC MT Battalion	Apr 46
		(Redesignated 11th MT Battalion Dec 44)	
1st Corps NC Battalion (53d NCB)	Dec 42	53d NC Battalion	Aug 46
1st Corps Signal Battalion	Jun 43	IIIAC Signal Battalion	Mar 46
IMAC Artillery	Apr 44	IIIAC Artillery	Oct 45
IMAC Transient Center	Jun 43	IIIAC Transient Center	May 44

14, 1944. During this period VAC controlled the 2d and 4th MarDivs and 7th and 27th InfDivs.

The two corps, IMAC/IIIAC and VAC, were raised and organized somewhat differently and initially assigned different missions. Their organic corps troops units were similar in allocation, but there were differences. How these units were employed also differed, as did their task organization for combat practices. The reason "Marine" was included in IMAC's designation and not in IIIAC's and VAC's was that IMAC was envisioned as essentially a Marine administrative command while IIIAC and VAC were intended as joint commands that could control Army units. IMAC units were redesignated as IIIAC units on April 15, 1944. Officially, corps units were designated, for example, MT Battalion, IIIAC.

Corps Defense Troops, VAC was activated in February 1944 on Hawaii to control defense battalions scattered through the Ellices, Gilberts, and Marshalls. Corps Defense Troops, IMAC was organized in March to control battalions in the Solomons. Both were deactivated in April and the defense battalions were reassigned to the new IIIAC and VAC Artillery organized on April 13. Corps Artillery would eventually control three each of 155mm howitzer and gun battalions as well as AAA battalions reorganized from the defense battalions. Corps Artillery, commanded by a brigadier-general, consisted only of a 117-man HQ battery plus attached battalions, which could include Army battalions.

The Amphibious Corps possessed an evolving service and administrative command arrangement for corps service troops and the various depots. Supply

The LVT(A)1 amphibian tank, armed with a 37mm gun, was first used at Roi-Namur. Its last use in action was at Peleliu, after which it was replaced by the 75mm howitzer-armed LVT(A)4. It had a 20mph on-shore speed and 7.5mph in the water.

V Amphibious Corps units, FMF/FMFPac	Activation/deactivation	Notes
VAC HQ&S Battalion	Sep 43–Feb 46	
VAC Medical Battalion	Mar 44–Jan 46	
VAC MT Company/Battalion	Jan 44–May 45	Bn Sep 44, remained company size
18th NC Battalion	Aug 42–Jun 45	
VAC Amphibious Recon Co/Bn	Aug 43–Aug 44	Bn Apr 44, to FMFPac Aug 44
VAC Signal Battalion	Aug 43–Feb 46	From 2d Corps Signal Bn
VAC Artillery	Apr 44–Jan 46	
VAC Transient Center	May 44–Jun 44	From IIIAC Transient Center, to FMFPac

An LVT(2) (foreground) and an LVT(1) lie disabled near the northwest tip of Betio, Tarawa Atoll. LVT(1) No. 49 was nicknamed *My Deloris* by the crew and was the first amtrac to reach shore. Today it is on display at the Tracked Vehicle Museum, Camp Pendleton, California.

The 2.5-ton DUKW-353 amphibian truck, or "Duck," made its debut with the Marines in February 1944 on Eniwetok Atoll. The six-wheel Duck could carry 25 troops or 5,000 lbs of cargo, or a 75mm or 105mm howitzer. One of its main roles was to haul artillery ammunition from ships to firing positions ashore.

Service, IMAC was organized on New Caledonia on May 20, 1943 to control the 1st and 4th Base and 2d and 3d Field Depots. On April 6, 1944 it was absorbed into Marine Supply Service, VAC. This command at Pearl Harbor had been raised on January 24, 1944 to support both VAC and IMAC. On April 10 it was redesignated Marine Administrative Command, VAC to provide supply, salvage, evacuation, construction, personnel management, quartering, sanitation, and other corps rear-echelon functions for IMAC (soon redesignated IIIAC) and VAC. It included Supply Service, Marine Administrative Command, VAC, which was formed by consolidating Supply Service, IMAC and Marine Supply Service, VAC. Marine Administrative Command, VAC was redesignated Administrative Command, FMF, Pacific and Marine Supply Command, VAC was redesignated Supply Service, FMF on June 14, 1944. Depots, service and supply battalions, and depot and ammunition companies were assigned to these commands.

Task organization for combat

The Marines task organized for combat into combined arms units with artillery, engineer, special troops, and service troops elements attached down to battalion and even company level. Support units were structured under a triangular reinforcement concept to allow equal attachments to combat units. With the infantry regiment as the basic unit for amphibious landings and combat ashore, divisional units were habitually attached to become regimental combat teams (RCT) or more commonly, combat teams (CT). During this period there was no standardized designation system for combat teams, which varied from division to division:

1st MarDiv	CT A (5th Marines), CT B (1st Marines), CT C (7th Marines)
2d MarDiv	CT 2, 3, 6
3d MarDiv	3d, 9th, 21st CT
4th MarDiv	RCT 23, 24, 25
1st MarBde	4th, 22d CT

Task-organized infantry battalions were called battalion landing teams (BLT) or simply landing teams (LT), identified by some combination of numbers indicating the battalion and parent regiment; for example, BLT3/1 for 3d Battalion, 1st Marines, and LT2/6 for 2d Battalion, 6th Marines.

Habitual attachments to a CT included: a 75mm pack howitzer battalion; tank, engineer, pioneer, amphibian tractor, MT, medical, and possibly Seabee companies; and a service and supply platoon and other detachments from the service battalion. An MP platoon might be attached to guard prisoners and direct traffic, and a section of the division band from the HQ company served as litter bearers. It is often assumed that platoons from these companies were then attached to BLTs. BLTs were kept lean with only small attachments, usually limited to tank and engineer platoons, a collecting section of the medical company supporting the regiment, and a shore fire-control party and an air-liaison team from the supporting joint assault signal company.

New organizational trends appeared during this period. More frequently the artillery battalions were retained under division control to provide fire to all regiments. In the past the division reserve regiment usually had fewer attachments, but now the trend was toward more balanced CTs although they were still sometimes referred to as the reserve group. Increasing numbers of small, specialized units began to be attached to CTs as they became available. Army units, especially amphibious tractor and amphibian truck, both of which the Marines were short of, were frequently attached to support Marine operations. The cross-attachment of artillery and AAA units between Marine

2d MarDiv task organization (Southern Landing Force), Tarawa, November 1943

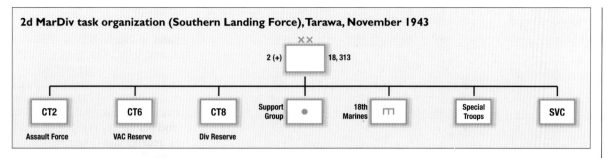

1st MarDiv task organization (Task Force BACKHANDER), New Britain, December 1943

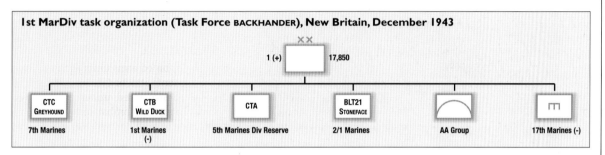

4th MarDiv task organization (Northern Troops and Landing Forces), Roi-Namur, January 1944

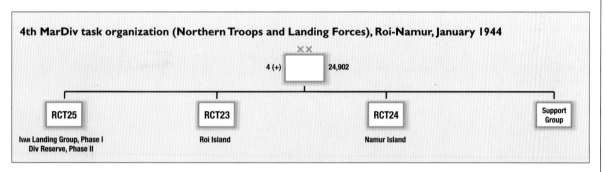

Tactical Group 1 task organization (Eniwetok Landing Forces), Eniwetok, February 1944

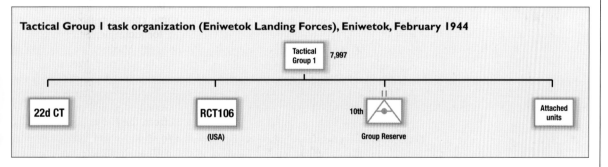

V Amphibious Corps task organization (Northern Troops and Landing Force), Saipan and Tinian, June 1944

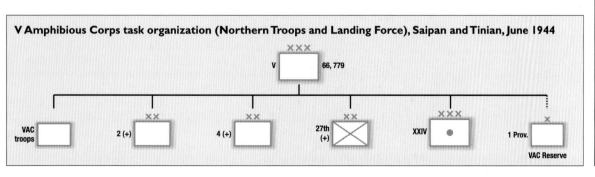

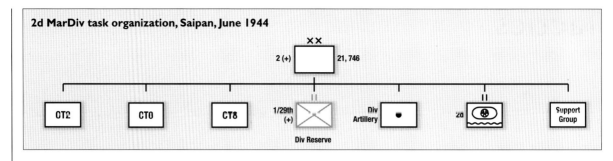

2d MarDiv task organization, Saipan, June 1944

××
2 (+) | 21, 746

CT2 — CT6 — CT8 — 1/29th (+) [Div Reserve] — Div Artillery — 2d — Support Group

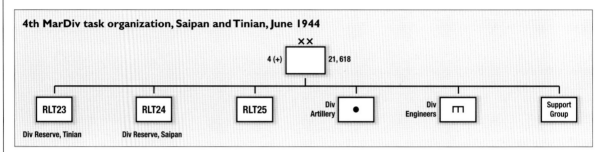

4th MarDiv task organization, Saipan and Tinian, June 1944

××
4 (+) | 21, 618

RLT23 [Div Reserve, Tinian] — RLT24 [Div Reserve, Saipan] — RLT25 — Div Artillery — Div Engineers — Support Group

and Army divisions became commonplace. Often, units were attached to battalions and regiments for embarkation and landing control, but would revert to regimental or division control soon after the landing.

The 1944 infantry battalion's organic elements were so organized that little cross-attachment was required within the unit. The rifle companies' machine-gun platoons had three two-gun sections, and a section was usually attached to each rifle platoon. A 37mm AT gun platoon from the weapons company might be attached to each battalion or kept under regimental control. A small aid station was attached to each rifle company from the battalion aid station.

Platoons were task organized for a landing. For example, the 4th MarDiv at Roi-Namur organized its platoons into an assault team and two boat teams, whether landed by LVT or LCVP. The 18–20-man assault team, led by the platoon leader, contained a machine-gun group (two LMGs from the machine-gun platoon), bazooka group, and demolitions group—the later two formed from a rifle squad. The assault team would advance ahead to clear defenses. The two boat teams were built around the other squads and platoon HQ troops. Once landed they would fight as teams until a lull allowed the platoon to consolidate.

Most divisions formed support groups to control the divisional special and service troops battalions minus their attachments to CTs as well as various attached corps units. As multiple-division operations occurred, various units were retained under corps control, especially artillery, AAA, non-divisional engineer and medical, and amphibian tractor. The latter were attached to specific regiments to support the landing, but once ashore they reverted to divisional or corps control. Anti-aircraft and amphibian tractor groups were formed to control these collected units.

Tactical Group 1, VAC and Task Group A, IMAC were formed on November 16, 1943 and February 22, 1944 respectively. These were essentially provisional brigades formed under the auspices of amphibious corps to conduct a specific, short-duration mission. They had no administrative duties, but were responsible for tactical operations and were experiments to test streamlined staffs and because sufficiently qualified staffs were not available to form brigades. They were built around a separate regiment with supporting units provided by division and corps troops.

Tactics

MacArthur's island-hopping concept was executed, which consisted of attacking the enemy where he was weak, by-passing his strongholds, and bombarding by-passed islands on which the enemy withered away. Tactical necessity and the lack of space for airfields on some islands sometimes required strongly held islands, such as Tarawa, to be seized. Most of the early Marine operations in the South Pacific involved landing unopposed or against light resistance on a large island that the Japanese did not occupy entirely. The Marines secured a perimeter within which a captured airfield was reconditioned and new ones built: they defended the perimeter against counterattacks, and then either conducted an offensive to clear the island (Guadalcanal, New Georgia) or contained the enemy and kept him away from the airfields (Bougainville, New Britain). These islands comprised dense jungle, swamps, and rugged interior mountains. Most actions were fought along the coasts. Marines may have conducted the initial landing, but the rest of the campaign was fought alongside Army divisions. Often the Army would continue the campaign, relieving the Marines to prepare for the next assault.

Airfields were the key to success in the Pacific. They were needed to support operations into adjacent island groups, as well as those within the same island group, to provide local defense, and to support the logistical effort. Fighters were short ranged and airfields helped maintain practical flying ranges. Aircraft carriers could provide some air support, but could not stay on-station indefinitely. Nor could they handle bombers and transports.

The November 1943 assault on Tarawa introduced a new kind of warfare. The Marines were forced to assault small, heavily defended islets comprising the Central Pacific atolls. The islands were low, generally level, and sparsely covered by palms and brush; the latter could be quite dense though, restricting observation, fire, and maneuver at the small-unit level. There was little room for either side to maneuver. Such was the situation in the Gilberts and Marshalls in late-1943 and early-1944. The summer of 1944 saw the US forces confronting a different kind of island. The Marianas were large islands (but smaller than those of the Solomons) featuring uplifted coral and limestone hills and ridges with vegetation varying from grass-covered plains, through dense scrub brush, to thick forests. Rather than being restricted to the coastal areas, operations would take place across the islands. The islands were large enough to allow both sides to maneuver, although the Japanese either failed to take advantage of this or were unable to do so because of American air superiority and the threat of air, artillery, and naval gunfire.

Amphibious assault

The assault of an island objective began months in advance, with submarines photographing the shorelines, air reconnaissance, the assembly of photographic mosaics and terrain models, the landing of reconnaissance teams, and the gathering of all available information from a variety of sources, including former residents and tourist books. Long-range bombers would pound the island and carrier raids would clear the objective and surrounding islands of aircraft and airfields. Air raids and submarines would sink or drive away ships in the area and cut it off from reinforcement. Battleship raids pounded the islands further. Eventually, in the early morning hours of D-Day, the invasion task force would arrive. Battleships, cruisers, and carrier aircraft would continue their attacks to keep the defenders under cover and prevent reserves from deploying to meet the

Underwater demolition teams (UDTs)
One of the key reasons why the Tarawa assault nearly failed was the lack of accurate intelligence on reefs, obstacles, and nearshore water conditions. It was vital to be able to destroy manmade and natural obstacles in order to allow landing craft to approach. The Navy formed its first UDTs in December 1943 using Navy, Army, and Marine personnel. First employed at Roi-Namur and Kwajalein in February 1944, the "frogmen" conducted pre-invasion hydrographic reconnaissance from the 3.5 fathom (21ft) curve to the high-water line. The UDTs located and destroyed obstacles, blasted boat lanes through reefs, marked boat lanes, and reported nearshore and beach conditions. The later 92-man UDTs comprised solely Navy personnel with many raised by assembling six-man Navy combat demolition units, Seabees, and others trained by the Joint Amphibious Scouts and Raiders School at Fort Pierce, Florida. All subsequent landings in the Pacific were preceded by UDT swimmers, armed only with a knife: they were instrumental in the success of landings. The Marines were supported by UDT-1 and -3 to -8 during 1944.

A 2d MarDiv rifle squad escorts an M4A2 tank as it passes through 27th InfDiv west-coast positions. These troops are mopping up after the *banzai* attack during the night of July 6/7, 1944, which signaled the beginning of the end of organized Japanese resistance on Saipan. The cliffs rising up to the Tanapag Plain are in the background.

landing. Underwater demolition team (UDT) frogmen would swim to shore and destroy obstacles and mines, blast gaps through reefs, and mark boat lanes. Fire-support landing craft, a new capability, would lead the assault waves to shore, laying down heavy, suppressive fire. These would halt outside the reef line and keep up their fire to the beachhead's flanks.

Landing control measures were much refined. Commanders had learned the value of effective and detailed landing rehearsals. This was especially important for ensuring fire support was effectively controlled. There were still instances where the lack of time and the dispersal of landing forces at various staging bases throughout the Pacific prevented complete rehearsals. The rehearsal sites often did not adequately portray conditions that would be found on the actual objective. Control boats, usually landing craft, control (LCC) or patrol craft (PC), were more effectively utilized to aid in the assembly and station-keeping of landing waves. A more flexible system of designating landing hours and days was established. While H-Hour and D-Day were still used, other letters were assigned frequently, as multiple landings would be accomplished on adjacent islands on different dates in the same area. A-, B-, W-, Y-, and Z-Hour and J- and W-Day were used in orders and radio traffic to prevent confusion between different landings.

The range of colors used to designate beaches was broadened and now included PURPLE, SCARLET, and BLACK along with the original RED, BLUE, GREEN, YELLOW, ORANGE, and WHITE. There might be up to four beaches of a given color additionally designated by a number, for example RED 1 through 4. Besides the main landing beaches, alternate or proposed beaches were designated. Sometimes these were used after the initial landing to bring ashore reserves or supplies. Normally a battalion was assigned to each beach with the same color identifying the beaches for a given regiment. The preferred beach was 1,000-plus yards wide, provided good approaches with few natural obstacles, and allowed easy exit from the beach toward the unit's objective. Most landings still occurred before 0900 hours, and while there were delays because of assembly problems or surf conditions, none were caused by enemy action.

The number of units that made up the initial assault depended on the availability of suitable landing beaches, strength and disposition of the defenders, inland terrain, location of initial objectives, and the island's size. While two or more possible landing sites may have been considered on a given

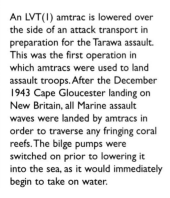

An LVT(1) amtrac is lowered over the side of an attack transport in preparation for the Tarawa assault. This was the first operation in which amtracs were used to land assault troops. After the December 1943 Cape Gloucester landing on New Britain, all Marine assault waves were landed by amtracs in order to traverse any fringing coral reefs. The bilge pumps were switched on prior to lowering it into the sea, as it would immediately begin to take on water.

island, the actual beaches selected depended on surf conditions, the extent of the defenses, and of great importance, proximity to a Japanese airfield. An existing airfield close to the beaches would be included within the beachhead and would be rapidly repaired by engineers and Seabees to allow close air support fighter-bombers to operate. The size of the landing force during this period varied from a single regiment to two divisions.

When assaulting atoll islands, the Marines landed on the lagoon side, inside the area enclosed by the ring of islets and the connecting submarine reef. The fringing reef stretching into the lagoon on this side of the island was much wider than on the ocean side. The Marines landed here because the surf was lighter, amtracs could carry troops across the reef, and Japanese defenses and obstacles were usually less developed. The Japanese had assessed that landings would occur on the ocean side, even though the surf was rougher, because the narrower reef allowed ramped landing craft to approach closer to shore. They were slow to reorient their defenses and appeared never to appreciate the capabilities of the large numbers of reef-crossing amtracs.

Two or more neighboring islets were usually secured prior to the main landing, on which up to four howitzer battalions were positioned. This ensured the availability of immediate fire support without having to wait for artillery to establish itself ashore. In small beachheads there was often insufficient room for artillery, and because of the short ranges they could not always provide effective indirect fire. Other islets flanking the lagoon's entrance would be secured as well.

A division preferably landed two regiments abreast on adjacent beaches with the third regiment in reserve. It would follow one of the assault regiments ashore within a few hours. A regiment's two assault battalions normally landed abreast with the third battalion coming ashore immediately behind one of the first. On small atoll islands usually only one regiment could land. With the exception of Tarawa, where the entire 2d MarDiv was committed, a regiment was large enough to secure the island. During multiple-division operations in the Marianas, the two divisions were landed some distance apart—up to seven miles in the case of Guam. Besides the initial inland objectives, a priority was to link up the two landing forces.

Amtracs were originally employed as cargo carriers. The Marines and the Army first used them to deliver assault troops across reefs impassable to landing craft in the Gilberts in November 1943. This became their primary mission and

Congested beachheads on the first day or two of an assault were a problem on most islands. There was insufficient room for artillery, supply dumps, aid stations, reserve units, and everything else that flowed ashore. This was even the case on Roi Island, where the assault battalions were able to push inland relatively quickly. In the background is an LCT(5), alongside which is an LCVP. On the left, at the water's edge, is a damaged LVT(A)1 amphibian tank.

A shore party unloads an LCT(5) from LCT Group 23 at Talasea, New Britain. By this date, sufficient shore-party personnel were allotted to unload landing craft. Prior to this, unloading operations were often undermanned.

later models were provided with armor plate and rear ramps. MajGen Holland Smith recommended that three amtrac battalions and an armored amtrac battalion support each Marine or Army division conducting an assault, totaling 312 cargo amtracs and 72 armored amtracs. An amtrac battalion could carry the assault elements of a regiment, and each amtrac company a battalion.

The armored amtracs constituted the first wave and would "shoot" the following assault waves ashore, maintaining a rapid rate of main gun and machine gun fire. While none too accurate on the water, it helped keep the enemy confined in their fortifications along with rocket, mortar, and gunfire from fire-support landing craft and last-minute strafing. Amphibian tanks would wade ashore and provide direct fire support to the following infantry until medium tanks were landed. Amphibian tanks were no substitute for tanks. Their armor was thin, they had a high profile, they were slow, and their narrow tracks and low ground clearance limited their cross-country mobility. Once tanks were landed the amphibian tanks provided mobile indirect fire support and beach security against counterlandings. The next four or so waves comprised troop-carrying amtracs landing assault troops. Subsequent waves would consist of landing craft with tanks, artillery, and support troops. The amtracs would come ashore and off-load their troops at the first available cover. They would immediately return to the transport area for additional troops or ammunition. After the initial assault, in which substantial numbers of amtracs might be lost, survivors would haul ammunition and supplies inland to the frontline, evacuate wounded and dead from the front under fire, tow artillery over rough terrain, create supply trails through forests, conduct beach and rear area security patrols, and be prepared to transport reconnaissance or rifle units to clear islets adjacent to the objective island.

Clearing the island

The time from when the landing occurred to when the island was declared secure could be anything from six hours (Roi) to two months (Saipan). Units were assigned objectives along the O-1 (Objective 1) Line to be secured before nightfall on D-Day. This was usually the first Marine-defendable line of terrain features close enough to the beaches to be reachable that day, but sufficiently inland to allow space in the beachhead for reserves, artillery positions, headquarters, supply dumps, aid stations, etc. Seldom was the complete O-1 Line achieved on D-Day, owing to the density of Japanese defenses around beaches. Subsequent O-lines were specified on which units focused on the following days, but these were more phase lines for tactical and logistical planning purposes, and may not have been completely secured on a given day. It was also possible that two or more O-lines might be overrun in a day.

The Navy preferred the Marines to land on the central part of an elongated island and then attack toward the opposite ends with the island cut in two. They felt this secured the island more quickly than landing on one end and attacking up the island's long axis. The Navy's motivation was to limit the time the invasion fleet was exposed to air and submarine attack. Available landing beaches often led the Marines to this scheme of maneuver—few suitable beaches were found on the ends of island—but it made their command and control, logistics, and fire support more complicated with forces attacking in opposite directions. An advantage of landing on one end of an island, if beaches were available, was that they usually had lighter infantry defenses and allowed

Casualties from Betio are floated out to the reef line aboard an LCR(L). From here they will be loaded on to landing craft and taken to troop transports, each of which operated a hospital.

the attackers to roll up the flanks of the beach defenses on the extended shores. Regardless, urgency was stressed at all echelons to secure the island as quickly as possible. This usually reduced casualties among assault troops.

Once the main Japanese defenses in the vicinity of the beaches had been overrun and the typically late and weak counterattacks defeated, assault troops drove inland to cut the island in two, isolate enemy pockets that may have withdrawn on to peninsulas, and secure airfields. The Japanese would establish stout and well-sited defense lines on key terrain, and these would be penetrated by close assault. The push would continue as the Japanese were driven to one or both ends of the island. Infantry–tank team coordination was essential. Tanks served as assault guns in direct support of the infantry using main guns, machine guns, and flamethrowers. A rifle squad was usually assigned to protect each tank from close-in attack. Infantry–tank training had been greatly emphasized and proved effective.

Small isolated enemy pockets, stragglers, and scattered groups would hide out in the rear areas while reserve units and service troops mopped up. Invariably the Japanese would attempt one final counteroffensive to drive the Americans from the island. Typically this would be insufficiently resourced and poorly coordinated, and would be defeated by massed American firepower. Some of these attacks were mass *banzai* charges resulting in the rapid destruction of the attackers. It was only a matter of time before the assault troops swept over a few remaining strongpoints at the far end of the island, and the cave in which the Japanese commander had committed suicide.

The island would be declared secure when organized resistance ceased. This was more than just a claim of victory. There was still significant mopping up to be done, even some pitched battles as last strongholds were overrun and stragglers conducted raids in American rear areas. This could go on for weeks. Once declared secure by the assault force commander, the island was turned over to the island command, an administrative organization controlling garrison troops, engineers, defense forces, and service troops who would remain to garrison the island and develop it as a naval, air, logistics, and troop staging base to support the next conquest. Certain combat units would remain on the island to complete the mopping up or fresh units might be brought in. A further mission was to clear other islets in the atoll or small adjacent islands where the Japanese had posted lookouts, or small defense forces, or where survivors from the main island objective had fled.

Fire support

Japanese survivors of the Pacific War have emphasized the effects of seemingly limitless American firepower. Marine and Army field artillery, naval gunfire, and close air support constituted the fire-support assets. This was supplemented by infantry mortars and AAA employed in the ground-fire role. Coordinating these diverse assets and ensuring they fired on the right targets at the right times using munitions appropriate for the targets was a major effort.

Field artillery included 75mm pack howitzers, 105mm howitzers, and 155mm howitzers and guns. The 75mm and 105mm were excellent for close fire in direct support of infantry. Battalions of both calibers were placed in direct support of infantry battalions, but their fire could be provided to any other infantry unit on a priority or need basis. The 155mm weapons provided deeper fire for counterbattery (attacking enemy artillery) and interdiction roles. The 155mm howitzers had a shorter range than the guns, but could more effectively attack targets on rear slopes of hills and ridges. The Marines were often criticized for sending in infantry to rout out the Japanese when heavy artillery fire could have softened up the defenders and reduced casualties. LtGen Holland Smith felt this was true and on July 1, 1944, after witnessing the limited use of artillery on Saipan, ordered that "massed artillery fires will be employed to support infantry attacks whenever practical."

The 75mm M1A1 pack howitzer remained the mainstay divisional artillery piece into 1945, with two or three battalions per division.

Mortars, which could provide rapid and responsive fire support to small units, were used sparingly on many of the smaller islands because of the small area and short duration of operations. This resulted in an underestimation of the quantity of mortar ammunition necessary for operations on the larger Mariana Islands.

Naval gunfire (NGF) was provided by destroyers, cruisers, and battleships using 5, 6, 8, 12, 14, and 16in. guns. NGF could provide a massive amount of accurate fire and had the advantage of being able to maneuver around the island and position itself for the best angle of attack. However, naval guns were designed to attack ships and had relatively flat trajectories. This made it difficult to attack targets on reverse slopes or to deliver plunging fire to penetrate bunker roofs. Early in the war, high-capacity, high-explosive ammunition, most effective for land targets, was in short supply, while armor-piercing rounds were plentiful. The latter were designed to penetrate heavy ship's armor, not layered logs, rocks, and sand. NGF could not always respond to fire requests as fast as field artillery, but this improved during the war. On Tarawa the NGF had been largely ineffective regardless of the weight of fire placed on the small island. The fire simply blanketed the island and shifted from area to area, resulting in few enemy killed and few fortifications knocked out. The wrong types of ammunition were used and ship-to-shore communications left much to be desired. This too improved. On Roi-Namur an estimated 50–75 percent of the enemy were killed in the pre-landing bombardment. NGF could also deliver star shells, which illuminated the ground in front of dug-in Marines at night. Field artillery and mortars could provide illumination as well, but the use of NGF for this purpose reduced the amount of illumination rounds that had to be brought ashore in lieu of high-explosive shells. The first sustained use of naval illumination was on Eniwetok.

An early problem was the NGF grid and target designation system used through the Gilberts campaign. It was sometimes cumbersome and inaccurate. A group of Army, Navy, and Marine officers at Pearl Harbor therefore developed the Tactical Area Designation System using a 1,000yd grid broken down into twenty-five 200yd lettered squares. This system was retained for the rest of the war by both field artillery and aviation to provide a common means of designating targets.

NGF relied on shipboard, aerial, and shore spotters. Each had its own advantages and limitations. It was found even before the war that Marine field artillery officers were capable of directing NGF. Ad hoc shore fire-control parties were formed from Navy personnel to accompany Marine units ashore and request NGF. Joint assault signal companies (JASCO) began to be established in October 1943 to provide shore- and beach-party communication, shore fire-control, and air-liaison parties and teams that were attached to divisional, regimental, and battalion headquarters. (JASCOs will be discussed in Battle Orders 8: *US Marine Corps Pacific Theater of Operations 1944–45*.)

Close air support provided by carrier- and land-based aircraft were considered equal partners with NGF. High-explosive bombs, semi-armor-piercing bombs for hardened targets, napalm bombs, rockets, and strafing proved effective if the ordnance was carefully matched with the target. Due to casualties caused by close air strikes, a policy of a "bomb safety line" 1,000yds forward of ground troops was adopted. The line could be brought in to 500yds when detailed control measures and coordination were practised. One of the main problems with close air support was the delay of one hour or more between the request and the delivery of ordnance. Sometimes the need for the strike had passed by the time the aircraft arrived, and it was directed against a secondary target.

Weapons and equipment

In late-1942 the Marine Corps began an aggressive program to update its weapons, and by early-1944 had been largely outfitted with new weapons. Most outdated weapons had been replaced by new models, and weapon production had sufficiently caught up with the demands of supplying the Army, Marines, and Allies. Most weapons unique to the Marines or of Navy origin had been replaced by standard Army weapons to ease logistical pressure. A concept of "units of fire" was adopted during the Central Pacific campaign to standardize and control ammunition supply. This provided a means of allocating ammunition. The number of rounds in a unit of fire varied depending on the type of weapon. In theory it was an average amount of ammunition that a weapon could expend in one day. Units might deploy with anything from three to five units of fire per weapon with additional ammunition loaded aboard ships.

Individual weapons

By late-1943 the semi-automatic .30-cal. M1 Garand rifle had replaced the bolt-action .30-cal. M1903 Springfield in most FMF units. Telescope-fitted '03s were used as sniper rifles and for a brief period one was retained in each rifle squad with an M1 grenade launcher. The M7 grenade launcher for the M1 rifle had not yet been widely issued. Springfields were still used by ships' detachments, Marine barracks and detachments guarding naval installations, and FMF service units.

The .30-cal. M1 carbine began to be widely issued to officers, weapons crewmen, radio operators, drivers, and headquarters and service personnel as a personal defense weapon. Not a single pistol was issued to members of infantry and artillery regiments, although .45-cal. M1911 and M1911A1 Colt pistols were assigned to other units. The carbine lacked knockdown power and penetration through vegetation, and sounded like the Japanese 6.5mm rifle. Few were used by rifle units other than by officers and heavy-weapon crewmen. The M8 grenade launcher for the carbine was issued in early-1944.

Thompson .45-cal. M1 and M1A1 SMGs began to be issued, although the heavier and more expensive M1928A1 remained in use. The new Thompsons had a 30-round magazine and could use the M1928A1's 20-round magazine, but not its 50-round drum. While only 49 SMGs were authorized in a division and none in infantry regiments, some found their way into line units, especially as a substitute for carbines among infantry leaders. One problem

A flamethrower operator with an M1A1 flamethrower assaults a simulated pillbox on a training course. By late-1943 the flamethrower had been improved and was considered an essential weapon by assault troops.

experienced with the Thompson was that it sounded like a Japanese 6.5mm light machine gun, causing a "Tommy-gunner" to draw friendly fire. Another was that the .45-cal. bullet, while a good man-stopper, had poor penetration through dense brush and bamboo.

The .45-cal. M50 and M55 Reising SMGs, and the Johnson .30-cal. M1941 rifle and M1941 LMG were withdrawn by late-1943; these weapons were found to be wanting, and standardization of weapons was desired. Reising guns remained in use by Marine naval station guards and ships' detachments.

The .30-cal. M1918A2 BAR remained the mainstay squad automatic weapon with the number in an infantry regiment almost doubling in 1944. This increased the number of BARs within a division, but those assigned outside of rifle companies were withdrawn. Infantry regiments retained a pool of 100 Winchester 12-gauge M97 and M12 pump-action riot shotguns. An example of the use of shotguns was their issue to half of G/2/8 for clearing Afetna Point on Saipan. Since they were attacking toward the flank of an adjacent unit, the scatterguns would be less dangerous to friendlies than longer-ranged rifles. The troops carried their M1s for later use.

Accompanying the new grenade launchers were a variety of rifle grenades to include M9A1 AT, M17 fragmentation, M19 white phosphorus, colored smoke, and colored-parachute and star-cluster flares for signaling. The number of grenade launchers was significantly increased in 1944, from one to nine per rifle squad. Hand grenades included the Mk IIA1 "pineapple" fragmentation, Mk IIIA1/A2 concussion, AN-M14 thermite incendiary, M15 white phosphorus, AN-M8 white smoke, and M16 and M18 colored smoke.

New assault demolition materials were fielded. Improved 20lb satchel charges with eight M3 or M4 C-2 plastic explosive blocks, hand-emplaced 10lb M2 shaped-charges for blasting pillboxes, and M1A1 bangalore torpedoes for blowing gaps through barbed wire and minefields were widely issued.

Crew-served infantry weapons

The .30-cal. Browning M1919A4 air-cooled LMGs and M1917A1 water-cooled HMGs remained in the Corps' inventory along with the Browning .50-cal. HB-M2 HMG (HB stands for "Heavy Barrel") as a unit AA weapon. As such the ".50-cals" were not assigned dedicated crews. These were sometimes manned by scratch crews for frontline use.

The improved 2.36in. M1A1 shoulder-fired rocket launcher (the bazooka) began to replace the M1 in late-1943 and came into wider use than the earlier model, but were still in short supply until early-1944. It weighed about the same as the M1, 13.2 lbs, and had the same 250yd range, but was more reliable.

The M1A1 backpacked flamethrower began to replace the M1. It was slightly more reliable, but weighed the same (70 lbs.) It had a longer range with thickened fuel (50yds), and 40yds with unthickened. The M1 was unable to use thickened fuel.

The 60mm M2 and 81mm M1 mortars still equipped rifle companies and infantry battalions, respectively. The 37mm M3A1 AT guns remained as equipment for regimental weapons companies. Though obsolete in Europe, they were still effective against Japanese tanks and were used to defeat pillboxes and *banzai* charges, the latter with canister rounds. The M3 and M3A1 halftrack-mounted 75mm SPM were still considered excellent AT weapons and assault guns for busting bunkers. The difference between the two models was the gun mount.

Artillery

The Marine division was still equipped with a mix of 75mm M1A1 pack howitzers and 105mm M2A1 howitzers. There was discussion of moving solely to the 105mm for its range and more lethal on-target effects and to eliminate one type of ammunition from the supply system. The 75mm was still useful in

A sand and olive drab-painted 155mm M1A1 "Long Tom" gun of the 10th Defense Battalion conducts practice firing in the anti-ship role. Note that the crew wears sand-colored helmets, which was not common. The gun normally had a 15-man crew. The battalion served as Eniwetok's garrison force.

that it could be carried in all landing craft and amtracs, was easy to off-load, could be manhandled into firing position without the need for prime movers, and could even be broken down into six loads to be carried over rough terrain for direct fire on caves and pillboxes. Its supporters argued that 75mm ammunition was still used in the 75mm howitzer-armed LVT(A)4 armored amtrac. The 105mm could be carried in the LVT(4) and the DUKW (if the wheels were replaced with narrowed truck wheels). The smallest landing craft that could carry it was the LCM. The 75mm was towed by a one-ton cargo truck and the 105mm by a 2.5-ton 6 x 6 truck.

The new FMF artillery battalions were equipped with 155mm M1A1 howitzers and M1A1 "Long Tom" guns, the latter being transferred from defense battalions. One could be landed in an LCM, but the landing craft, tank (LCT) was more commonly used as it could accommodate two guns, a prime mover, and ammunition. Prime movers were the 2.5-ton short-wheelbase cargo truck and 18-ton M4 high-speed tractor, respectively. The few units still assigned a coast defense mission were mostly armed with the Long Tom, but fixed defense forces on Samoa, Midway, and Johnston retained the old 3, 5, 6, and 7in. guns.

Weapon	Max Effective Range	Rate of Fire
75mm M1A1 pack howitzer	9,610yds	6 rpm
105mm M2A1 howitzer	12,300yds	2–4 rpm
155mm M1A1 howitzer	12,700yds	1–3 rpm
155mm M1A1 gun	25,715yds	1–3 rpm

The earlier 3in. M3, 37mm M1, and .50-cal. M2 water-cooled AA weapons were almost completely replaced by the 90mm M1A1, 40mm M1, and twin 20mm Mk 4 AA guns. These weapons were often employed against ground targets to supplement field artillery fire. They were supported by several radar systems including the SCR-268 for fire control and the SCR-270D and 602 long-range warning radars. The SCR-602 was a lightweight version better suited for amphibious operations than the 270. In mid-1944 the cumbersome 270 was replaced by the more portable SCR-584.

A new weapon entering the Marine inventory in 1943 was the 4.5in. barrage rocket. It saw limited use with the 1st Corps Experimental Rocket Platoon on Choiseul, Bougainville, and Guam. The platoon was armed with the first 2.36in. M1 bazookas received by the Corps and 4.5in. T27E1 launchers. This was a single-tube, man-portable tube fired from a collapsible tripod. It merely fired one rocket at a time and, being comparatively inaccurate, proved to be

The 90mm M1A1 anti-aircraft gun served defense battalions and anti-aircraft artillery battalions. The Marine Corps' key AA weapon, it had an 11,273yd vertical range and a 25 rounds-per-minute rate of fire.

| Marine tanks 1943–44 | | |
Model	Armament	Employed
M3A1	flame gun, 3 × .30-cal. MG	1943–44
M3A3	37mm gun, 3 × .30-cal. MG	1943–44
M5	37mm gun, 3 × .30-cal. MG	1943–44
M5A1	37mm gun, 3 × .30-cal. MG	1943–44
M4A1	75mm gun, 2 × .30-cal., 1 × .50-cal. MG	1942–43
M4A2	75mm gun, 2 × .30-cal., 1 × .50-cal. MG	1942–45
M4A3	75mm gun, 2 × .30-cal., 1 × .50-cal. MG	1944–50
M32B1/B2*	81mm mortar, 1 × .30-cal., 1 × .50-cal. MG	1944–50

*The M32B1/B2 recovery vehicle mounted an 81mm mortar for smoke screening.

ineffective as it did not offer a high-volume, area barrage capability. The new rocket detachments of 1944 were armed with the Navy Mk 7 launcher, which the Army called the T45. This was a gravity-fed launcher rack, designed for fire-support landing craft, holding 12 rockets. Three racks were mounted in the rear of a one-ton cargo truck, nicknamed the "Handy Andy" after a popular toy, and electrically fired. First used on Saipan, they proved to be effective area fire weapons capable of launching 36 high-explosive and white-phosphorus rockets in four seconds to a range of 1,100yds.

Tanks

The 37mm gun-armed M2A4, M3, and M3A1 light tanks, with which the Marines had fought in the Solomons, had been replaced by the M3A3, M5, and M5A1 by late-1943. Even though the Marines encountered comparatively "larger" Japanese tank forces on some islands, the Marines still far outclassed them in capabilities and tactics. Due to this, the Marines still employed tanks largely in the infantry support role. 75mm gun-armed M4 Sherman medium tanks began to replace most 37mm-armed light tanks in early-1944, and they proved especially useful in the assault-gun role. By the spring of 1944 most light tanks had been replaced by Shermans. Limited use was made of the M4A1 with the A2 and A3 seeing much wider service. By the end of 1944 the M4A3 had replaced the A2 in all but the 1st and 3d tank battalions.

M5A1 light tanks await the order to advance inland on Namur. This operation saw the last widespread use of light tanks by the Marines. These tanks are fitted with LT-5 stack fording kits. This kit allowed a tank to wade through 6ft of water. Release cables allowed the stacks to be easily discarded once ashore. The tanks' camouflage colors are dark green and sand.

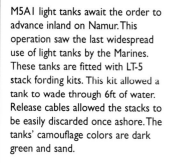

M3A1 tanks of Company B, 1st Light Tank Battalion advance through a coconut plantation in support of 2d Battalion, 158th Infantry at Arawe on the south coast of New Britain. This was one of several occasions when Marine tanks supported Army units in the Southwest Pacific.

On Saipan M3A1s mounted an A-H1B "Satan" flamegun in lieu of the main gun with a 40–60yd range. Its 170 gallons of fuel gave it 120 seconds of fire, usually fired in short bursts.

Command, control, communications, and intelligence

Command and control

Command and staff procedures had changed somewhat since 1942. There were numerous refinements in the planning process, information flow, and logistical planning. The manning of headquarters at all echelons from company up was increased to distribute the work load more effectively, allow more efficient 24-hour operations, and assign additional staff specialists to handle specialized actions. The originally small engineer, medical, and tank battalion headquarters companies provided only minimal control as their subordinate companies were habitually attached to CTs. In 1944 these were enlarged to provide expanded support.

Besides the principal staff officers (1—Personnel, 2—Intelligence, 3—Operations and Training, 4—Supply, and 5—Plans [division and higher]) found at battalion through FMF levels, there were numerous special staff officers who increased in number at each higher echelon. Principal staff officers and sections were identified by a letter preceding their numeric designation: Bn—Battalion, R—Regiment, B—Brigade, D—Division, A—Corps Artillery, C—Amphibious Corps, F—FMFPac.

Infantry Regiment and Battalion Command and Staff Officers

Regiment Assignment	Rank	Battalion Assignment	Rank
Regimental Commander	Col	Battalion Commander	LtCol
Executive Officer	LtCol	Executive Officer	Maj
R-3	Maj	Bn-3	Maj
Chemical Officer	Capt	Chemical Officer	Lt
Asst R-3, Regimental Demolitions Officer	Lt		
R-4	Maj	Bn-4	Capt
Asst R-4, Maint & MT Officer	Lt		
Asst R-4, Ordnance & Munitions Officer	Lt		
R-1, Adjutant	Capt	Bn-1, Adjutant	Lt
Asst R-1	Lt		
Asst R-1, Classification Officer	Lt		
R-2	Capt	Bn-2	Lt
Asst R-2	Lt		
Asst R-2, Aerial Photo Interpretation	Lt		
Communication Officer (also Communication Platoon Commander)	Maj	Communication Officer (also Communication Platoon Commander)	Lt
Paymaster (also Paymaster Section Commander)	Maj		
Quartermaster (also Service Platoon Commander)	Capt		
Liaison Officers (x2)	Lt		

Notes: additionally, the regiment had two Navy Medical Corps surgeons, a Dental Corps officer, and two Chaplain Corps officers whose ranks were not specified in the T/O. There were two Navy Medical Corps surgeons in the battalion.

The Commandant of the Marine Corps, LtGen Alexander A. Vandegrift, confers with MajGen Charles D. Barrett, Commanding General, IMAC, on Guadalcanal, 1944. A large Marine staging base had been developed at Tassafarougu west of Henderson Field, which was used by the divisions during their later operations.

An SCR-300 walkie-talkie-equipped radio operator, accompanying a rifle company command group on Saipan, shelters behind an M4A2 tank mounting an MT-S stack fording kit that has not yet been jettisoned. Over the left rear fender is a jury-rigged field telephone allowing infantrymen to communicate with the tank crew.

Corps special staff officers included: Air, Artillery, Engineer, Headquarters Commandant, Liaison, LVT, Medical, NGF, Ordnance, Public Relations, Shore Party, Signal, and Transport Quartermaster. At lower echelons many of these special staff duties were handled as additional duties ("double-billeted" or "dual-hatted") by other headquarters officers.

Communication elements at all echelons were enlarged and additional radios assigned to provide expanded command and control and to speed the passing of information and requests. Expanded radio nets were developed providing dedicated nets (with their own assigned frequencies) for command, intelligence, fire support, air support, logistics, administration, etc.

Communications

Marine units, which had only small amounts of radio equipment at the beginning of the war, had by 1944 increased the numbers and types of radios. Besides the Navy radios with which the Corps began the war, more use was made of Army radios. T/Os did not specify the numbers or types of radios. The 1944 infantry T/O only specified eight jeep-mounted TCS radios, scattered between the regimental and battalion communication platoons and regimental weapons company. The latter also had SCR-510 radios in the four 75mm SPMs. Other radios were issued as described below, but their types and numbers varied over time and between units.

Besides equipping regimental and battalion headquarters as semi-fixed and fixed stations, amtracs, reconnaissance vehicles, and landing craft were fitted with the TCS-1 to 14 semi-portable radio. The different variants covered different frequency ranges (for example, frequencies used by infantry and artillery units) or were modifications. The frequencies overlapped to some extent to permit intercommunication between different types of units. There were instances when different units had communications problems due to frequency mismatch. This situation improved though as new versions of the radios were fielded with broader frequency ranges and increased use of Army radios. The TCS was capable of voice or Morse Code and was considered an excellent radio, as its 120-plus lb weight was not an issue when mounted in vehicles.

At company level were the TBY-1 and TBY-2 ultra-portable radios, which were 37 lb backpacked models capable of voice and Morse Code on line-of-sight. Six TBYs were also allocated at battalion level and a few at regimental level to allow short-range voice communications with subordinate units. Other battalion and regimental-level radios were the TBX-1 to TBX-6. These were man-portable radios, but could not be operated on the march. It required three men to man-pack the 29 lb transmitter-receiver, 31 lb accessory box with receiver batteries, 22 lb hand-cranked generator for transmitter power, and wire antenna. While capable of voice communications, they were usually used only for Morse Code. It required at least 15 minutes to set up, transmit a message, and breakdown. A major complaint of the TBX was that it was inadequately waterproofed. It was recommended in late-1943 that it be replaced with the equivalent Army radio, the SCR-284, but the TBX remained in use into late-1944. By late-1943 a radio was provided to platoon leaders with a couple in the company headquarters. This was the MU, a lightweight battery-operated set that was carried in a canvas case by a shoulder strap. Its frequency range did not allow it to talk to TBYs at company level. It proved too fragile and the batteries had a short life. Shore party elements were provided with the 5.5 lb RBZ radio receiver. This was a small, compact receiver carried in a canvas chest bag. Its earphones were fitted in a skull cap, which allowed it to be worn under the steel helmet with a wire lead clipped to the helmet making it the antenna. It allowed elements ashore to receive instructions and air-raid warning alerts transmitted from ships. Two Army radios that came into wide use at company and platoon levels in mid-1944 were the SCR-300 "walkie-talkie," a backpack model, and the handheld 5 lb SCR-536 "handy-talkie." The SCR-300 weighed about 35 lbs and had a range of some 3 miles. The SCR-536 had less than a one-mile range. On Tinian SCR-300s were given to tank platoon commanders, allowing them to communicate directly with the infantry they supported.

Some 400 Navajo code talkers served in the Marine Corps, with the first recruited in March 1942. Trained as radio operators, they developed a 600-word code vocabulary substituting Navajo words for English ones. Navajo lacked modern military terms, and so Navajo words were assigned to English military terms, thus making radio messages impossible to translate, even if the Japanese had had anyone able to understand Navajo—there were fewer than 30 non-Navajos, mainly missionaries, who could understand the language. The code talkers would verbally transmit the message in Navajo code with the receiving code talker simply writing it in English on a message pad. First used on Guadalcanal, most commanders initially failed to understand the concept and simply used them as regular radio operators or messengers.

Field telephones were still widely used, both the Marine Corps MCT-1 and the Army EE-8. The 46-man 1st–6th Separate Wire Platoons had been organized in 1943 to augment divisional wire laying and repair capabilities. Messenger dogs came into use when the 1st–6th Marine War Dog Platoons were fielded, with their first use on Bougainville in November 1943. The 62-man platoons had a scout dog section with 18 handlers and dogs. The messenger dog section had 18 dogs (mostly German Shepherds) and 36 handlers. One handler would accompany the forward unit he was attached to while the other remained at the higher headquarters with the dog dispatched back and forth between them.

MajGen Holland M. Smith ("Hollin' Mad Smith") had a fiery reputation, but his drive and ability to get things done made him the first commanding general of Fleet Marine Force, Pacific. FMFPac controlled all Marine combat and aviation units in the Pacific Theater.

Intelligence

The Marine Corps' emphasis on military intelligence was admittedly weak at the beginning of the war. This was partly due to commanders' past experience in only small-unit actions against bandits and guerrillas during the Latin American "Banana Wars" and reliance on the Navy for higher-level intelligence. One of the principal defects was a failure in receiving and passing detailed battlefield intelligence information in a timely manner. This also applied to the often dismal record of higher commands passing information to subordinate units. It would not be until 1944 that information was routinely and effectively passed to Marine units.

Members of a Joint Intelligence Center/Pacific Ocean Area prisoner-of-war interrogation team with Japanese prisoners on the Iboki Plantation, New Britain. Col John T. Selden, CO, 5th Marines (standing with jacket open) observes proceedings. Once captured, Japanese prisoners often volunteered information. Interrogations had to be conducted as soon as possible after capture in order to exploit any tactical information gathered.

The Navy's Intelligence Center/Pacific Ocean Area (ICPOA) at Pearl Harbor was the principal theater intelligence collection, analysis, and distribution organization. It was expanded and redesignated by adding the prefix "Joint" to its title in September 1943. Almost 2,000 Navy, Army, and Marine personnel were assigned to JICPOA. Marines were mainly assigned to the Enemy Land Section for order of battle analysis, analyzed enemy weapons, and studied Japanese island defenses. Among the most notable intelligence achievements accomplished by JICPOA was an accurate photo analysis of Roi-Namur, allowing NGF to inflict a great deal of damage, and accurate hydrographic

analysis at Kwajalein, Saipan, Tinian, and Guam. JICPOA also provided interrogation teams (comprising Japanese–Americans) and enemy material and salvage teams that accompanied Marine units during landings.

The most important intelligence to the Marines was enemy order of battle, strengths of the different categories of troops, locations and calibers of heavy weapons, locations and types of defenses, obstacles, beach and nearshore water conditions, and the terrain hidden beneath jungle canopies. Most of this information was acquired through aerial and submarine photography and communications intercepts of Japanese coded radio traffic, which had been broken by the ULTRA system.

Tactical intelligence was obtained through aerial photography. Since maps were seldom available of objective islands, updated aerial photos were continuously issued to ground units as bombardment stripped away vegetation, revealing more to the camera and changing the face of the battlefield. An aerial photograph interpretation officer was assigned to the R-2 Section in the light of the importance of this.

Division reconnaissance companies had a key role in battlefield information collection, but they were also used to clear islets adjacent to the objective island, secure gaps between units with outposts and patrols, to conduct rear area mopping up, employed as a reserve, or to secure the division command post. The April 4, 1944 F-89 T/O called for a 132-man company with a 28-man headquarters and three 33-man recon platoons. The platoon headquarters had a lieutenant platoon leader, chief scout (gunnery sergeant doubling as platoon sergeant), platoon guide (platoon sergeant—his rank), radio maintenance sergeant (staff sergeant), three radio operators (corporal, two PFC/privates), photographer (corporal), rubber boat man (corporal), two "other duty" PFC/privates, and a Navy Corpsman (pharmacist's mate 2d class). The three recon squads had a squad leader (sergeant), assistant squad leader (corporal), automatic rifleman (PFC/private), and four scouts (PFC/privates). All hands were armed with the M1 carbine except the rubber boat man, other duty privates, and scouts who had M1 rifles, and the automatic riflemen with BARs. Having given up their jeeps, transport was on foot or in rubber boats.

The regimental scout and sniper platoon was deleted in 1944, but the regimental intelligence section possessed a 15-man scout and observer squad (one sergeant, four corporals, 10 PFC/privates). Two scout and observer corporals and seven PFC/privates were assigned to the battalion intelligence section. The scouts and observers, all armed with M1 rifles, had existed previously and besides conducting reconnaissance patrols or accompanying other units' patrols, assisted the R-2 and Bn-2 as necessary. Prior to the 1944 reorganization it was proposed to eliminate the scout company and reassign the personnel to the divisional, regimental, and battalion intelligence sections for increased organic reconnaissance capabilities.

From 1943 divisional reconnaissance companies had no organic vehicles other than the ten-man landing craft, rubber (large), or LCR(L). This was 14ft 8in. long, and 7ft 9in. wide. Besides paddles, it could be fitted with a 9.5hp Evinrude outboard motor, giving it a speed of 3.4–4.5 knots.

Combat operations

Unit status

The 1st and 2d MarDiv's final battles of 1943 were the last that witnessed the establishment of a lodgment perimeter on a large island without clearing the entire island (New Britain), and the first to be fought on a small atoll (Tarawa) against heavy defenses. Besides reorganizations, new weapons and new equipment, a wealth of lessons had been learned from vicious combat, and these were integrated into training and planning at all levels. The beginning of 1944 found the Marine Corps with three experienced divisions—the 1st (Guadalcanal, New Britain), 2d (Guadalcanal, Tarawa), and 3d (Bougainville).

The 1st MarDiv was engaged on New Britain, having landed at the end of 1943. The Division would suffer comparatively light casualties there, fewer than experienced on Guadalcanal or Bougainville. It would suffer heavily though from the harsh environment with large numbers of troops affected by disease and weather injuries. After its relief in April 1944, it would move to the Russells for rebuilding and would not be committed again until September 1944 on Peleliu. The 2d MarDiv was on Hawaii rebuilding from Tarawa and preparing for Saipan. Its 6th Marines was still garrisoning Tarawa and would remain until February. The 3d MarDiv had returned to Guadalcanal in January 1944 having been relieved from Bougainville to rebuild and prepare for Guam.

In January 1944 the new 4th MarDiv was en route to the Marshalls for its first assault. It had departed California and would sail 4,300 miles directly to its objective, making it the longest amphibious assault transit in history (until the 8,000-mile 1982 British Falklands expedition). The separate 22d Marines would serve as a reserve in this operation and the new 4th Marines was organized from the raider battalions in February.

The divisions undergoing rest, rebuilding, and retraining had to absorb lessons learned, new doctrine, new equipment, and replacements. Integrating replacements often proved difficult, not merely because of the difficulties of acceptance by veterans, but because they had to learn their new jobs and work hard to become part of the team. There were internal reorganizations within units as changes to T/Os were implemented, as well as officers and NCOs reassigned to new billets. With often new commanders and staffs at all echelons from squad to division, headquarters had to work hard to develop command relationships and procedures. One main difficulty was convincing veterans, who had previously undergone long unit training and been molded by combat into smoothly functioning teams, to take retraining seriously.

Bismarcks and Central Pacific Operations			
Island	Island Codename	Operation Codename	Marine Participation
Tarawa	INCREDIBLE	LONGSUIT	20 Nov 43–4 Dec 43 (14 days)
New Britain	ARABIC	BACKHANDER	26 Dec 43–1 Mar 44 (121 days)
Roi-Namur	BURLESQUE-CAMOUFLAGE	FLINTLOCK	31 Jan 44–2 Mar 44 (32 days)
Eniwetok	DOWNSIDE	CATCHPOLE	17 Feb 44–2 Mar 44 (14 days)
Saipan	TATTERSALLS	FORAGER	11 Jun 44–10 Aug 44 (60 days)
Tinian	TEARAWAY	FORAGER	24 Jul 44–10 Aug 44 (17 days)

Assault troops storm one of the large bombproof bunkers behind Beach RED 3 on Tarawa. The men in the upper right are putting grenades into a T-shaped air vent.

Veterans were disinterested in conducting basic unit exercises to integrate green replacements—they had done it all before.

Tarawa

The Gilberts (OVERFED) assault would be the first Allied foray into the Central Pacific. The Gilberts are 2,400 miles southwest of Hawaii and 2,800 miles northeast of Australia. The Gilberts' 16 widely scattered atolls and islands were a British Crown Colony occupied by Japan in December 1941. There was only a minor presence until the August 17–18, 1942 raid by the 2d Raider Battalion on Makin Island, Butaritari Atoll. The Japanese then extensively reinforced Tarawa and Butaritari with Special Naval Landing Forces (SNLF). The Ellice Islands, 460 miles southeast of Tarawa, were occupied by the Marines between October 1942 and August 1943. Bomber bases on these islands supported operations in the Gilberts.

The Japanese built only one airstrip in the Gilberts, discovered by the US in January 1943—Tarawa Atoll. Its capture was essential to provide an airfield within range of Kwajalein Atoll in the Marshalls 550 miles to the northwest. Operation LONGSUIT tasked the Marines with seizing Tarawa (INCREDIBLE) and the Army Butaritari (KOURBASH) 105 miles to the north, the northernmost of the Gilberts and the only other defended atoll, though less stoutly so than Tarawa.

Tarawa is a triangular atoll with 42 islets on its 12-mile southern base and 18-mile northeast side; the open west side is devoid of islands. The objective

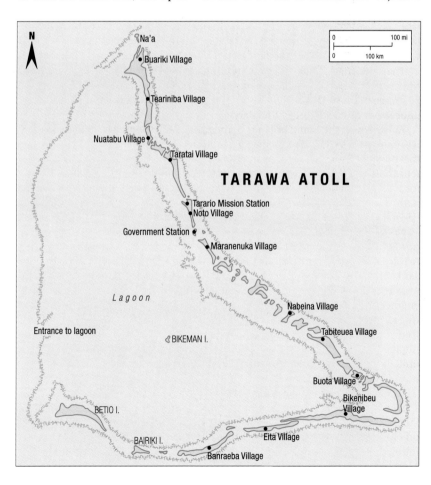

Tarawa Atoll, Gilbert Islands, November 1943.

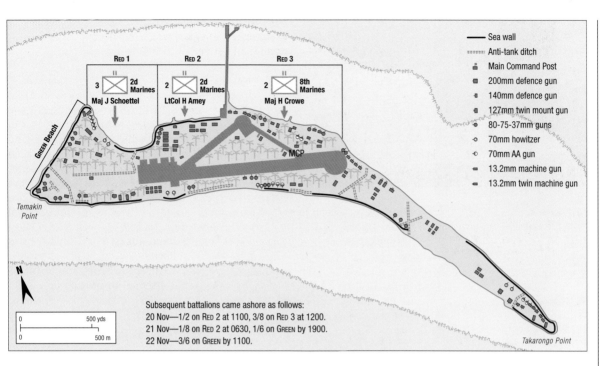

H-Hour (0845), D-Day, Betio Island, Tarawa Atoll, November 20, 1943.

was Betio (HELEN) on the west end of the atoll's south arm. It is 800yds across its west end and tapers to a point at its opposite end 3,800yds east. Covered with palms with an elevation of 10ft, it was surrounded by a 3–5ft coconut log seawall. A 500–1,000yd-wide fringing reef surrounds the island. The 1,600ft Government ("Long" or "Central") Pier extended from the north-central shore.

The 4,866 men of the 3d Special Base Force, Sasebo 7th SNLF, and construction troops were dug into 500 log, concrete, and steel pillboxes and bunkers, with 82 antiboat, coast defense, and AA guns from 37mm to 200mm caliber as well as underwater obstacles ringed the island.

Air strikes on the island began in September 1943. The 17,447-man 2d MarDiv, reinforced to 18,313 (Southern Landing Force) under VAC, was tasked with the mission. The Division departed Wellington, New Zealand and conducted rehearsals at Efaté, New Hebrides. The Southern Attack Force (Task Force 53) sailed for the Gilberts on 13 November to arrive pre-dawn on the 20th (D-Day). Naval bombardment began and the first landing waves went in to land at 0845 (H-Hour), led, for the first time, by amtracs.

Much effort had been expended to acquire additional amtracs including new LVT(2)s and to add boilerplate armor. These were assigned to Company A-1 comprising personnel drawn from 1st and 2d Amphibian Tractor, 2d Light Tank, and 2d Special Weapons battalions. Small numbers of 2.36in. M1 bazookas were issued, but training was inadequate. M1A1 flamethrowers were issued to the engineer battalion with a 4–6-man flamethrower and demolition team attached to each rifle platoon of the CTs' 2d and 3d Battalions. The CTs' 1st Battalion were the reserve and had bomb disposal squads attached for mine clearing. Augmenting each CT was a D-2 photographic detachment, a Navy air-warning unit, four air liaison detachments, and four shore fire-control parties (one to each CT, one to each LT).

Beaches RED were on the northwestern shore of Betio. LT3/2 landed on RED 1 near the west end. The remainder of CT2 landed on RED 2 west of the Long Pier. LT2/8, attached to CT2, landed on RED 3 east of the Long Pier and centered on either side of the 150ft Burns Philip Pier 400yds east of the Long Pier. It was followed by 3/8, also attached to CT2, landing on RED 3 as reinforcements. Most troops landing after 1000 hours were brought in by landing craft and

An SNLF sailor is escorted to the beach by MPs for evacuation. In the background, support troops stare at one of the few living Japanese they have seen. Only 17 were captured on Betio.

halted at the reef lip by the unexpected lower than normal tide and forced to wade 500–1,000yds across the fire-swept reef. HQ, 8th Marines and its 1/8 landed on RED 2 on D+1. LT1/6 landed using rubber boats on Beach GREEN on the island's west end on D+1 to be followed by 3/6 on D+2. LT2/6 had previously cleared Bairiki (SARAH) 3,000yds to the east of Betio, landing on Beach BLUE. 2/10 landed on Bairiki on D+2 to provide fire support while 3/10 fired from Eita (ELLA) 5,500yds to the east. Commander of the 2d MarDiv had desired to land artillery on these islets prior to the main landing to provide fire support, which may have helped the hard-pressed Marines trapped behind the seawall under withering fire, but this was denied by the naval commander as it was thought it would prolong the operation. The Navy feared massive air attacks from the Marshalls, which never materialized. Pushing to the island's east end Betio was declared secure at 1321, November 23 after a 76-hour fight. The Marines suffered over 3,000 casualties and the Japanese force was virtually wiped out with only 158 prisoners taken. Out of 125 LVTs, 35 were lost, as were 12 of the 14 M4A2 tanks landed in Wave 5, the only use of 1st Corps Tank Battalion (Medium) Shermans in combat.

Tarawa's other islets were cleared by LT2/6 and Company D (Scout), 2d Light Tank Battalion between November 21–28. On the 21st a Japanese company on Bairiki escaped to Buariki at the atoll's north end to be wiped out on the 26th.

2d MarDiv (Reinforced) (Southern Landing Force)
Combat Team 2 (Assault Force)
2d Marines (Reinforced)
Landing Team 2/8 (- Battery H, 3d Battalion, 10th Marines)
1st Battalion, 10th Marines [artillery]
Battery O, 5th Battalion, 10th Marines
Special Weapons Group, 2d Defense Battalion
Company C, 1st Corps Tank Battalion (Medium) [M4A2]
Company A (- 1st Platoon; + 3d Platoon, Co C), 1st Battalion [engineer], 18th Marines
Company D, 2d Battalion [pioneer], 18th Marines
Detachment, HQ&S Company, 2d Amphibian Tractor Battalion
Company A, 2d Amphibian Tractor Battalion [LVT(1)]
Special Amphibian Tractor Detachment (aka Company A-1) [50 x LVT(2)]
Company A, 2d Medical Battalion
1st Platoon, 1st MP Company
Detachment, HQ, 2d Battalion [pioneer], 18th Marines
Detachment, HQ, 3d Battalion [NC], 18th Marines
Detachment, HQ&S Company, 18th Marines
Detachment, 1st Ordnance Company, 2d Service Battalion
Detachment, 1st Platoon, S&S Company, 2d Service Battalion
1st Band Section
Combat Team 6 (VAC Reserve—released to 2d MarDiv 1421, D-Day)
6th Marines (Reinforced)
2d Battalion, 10th Marines [artillery]
5th Battalion (- Battery O), 10th Marines
Company B, 2d Amphibian Tractor Battalion [LVT(1)]
Company B, 2d Light Tank Battalion [M3A1]

(continued on page 53)

Company B, 2d Medical Battalion

Company B, 1st Battalion [engineer], 18th Marines

Company E, 2d Battalion [pioneer], 18th Marines

Battery A, 2d Special Weapons Battalion

2d Platoon, 1st Military Police Company

Detachment, HQ, 1st Battalion [engineer], 18th Marines

Detachment, HQ&S Company, 18th Marines

Detachment, 2d Ordnance Company, 2d Service Battalion

Detachment, 2d Platoon, S&S Company, 2d Service Battalion

Detachment, 2d Signal Company

2d Band Section

Combat Team 8 (Division Reserve)

8th Marines (Reinforced) (- LT2/8)

3d Battalion, 10th Marines [artillery]

Company C, 2d Light Tank Battalion [M3A1]

Company C, 2d Medical Battalion

Company C (- 3d Platoon; + 1st Platoon, Co A), 1st Battalion [engineer], 18th Marines

Company F, 2d Battalion [pioneer], 18th Marines

Company C (-), 2d Amphibian Tractor Battalion [LVT(1)]

3d Platoon, 1st MP Company

Detachment, HQ, 1st Battalion [engineer], 18th Marines

Detachment, 3d Platoon, S&S Company, 2d Service Battalion

Detachment, 3d Ordnance Company, 2d Service Battalion

3d Band Section (-)

Support Group

10th Marines (-) [artillery]

    HQ&S Battery (-), 10th Marines

    3d and 4th Battalions, 10th Marines

18th Marines (-) [engineer]

Detachment, HQ&S Company, 18th Marines

Companies H and I, 3d Battalion [NC], 18th Marines

Special Troops

HQ, 2d MarDiv (-)

2d MP Company (-)

2d Signal Company (-)

    HQ&S Company (-), 2d Light Tank Battalion

Company D (Scout), 2d Light Tank Battalion

Detachment, 3d Band Section

Party, HQ, VAC

Service Troops

Detachment, HQ&S Company, 2d Medical Battalion

Company E, 2d Medical Battalion

Company A, 2d MT Battalion

Detachments, Ordnance Company, 2d Service Battalion

Detachments, S&S Company, 2d Service Battalion

A Marine sketches the details of a Japanese steel portable pillbox on Betio, the only island on which they were encountered. They were shipped to the island in sections and assembled there. The pillboxes were double-walled, with a 12in. gap between the walls that was filled with sand. (See Fortress 1: *Japanese Pacific Island Defenses 1941–45*.)

Marine Commanders, Gilberts

V Amphibious Corps	**MajGen Holland M. Smith**
Chief of Staff	BGen Graves B. Erskine
VAC HQ and Service Battalion	Maj Thomas R. West
2d Defense Battalion	Col Norman E. True
one-half 2d Airdrome Battalion	LtCol Thomas G. McFarland
2d Marine Division	**MajGen Julian C. Smith**
Assistant Division Commander	BGen Leo D. Hermle
Chief of Staff	Col Merritt A. Edson
2d Marines	Col David M. Shoup
1st Battalion	Maj Wood B. Kyle
2d Battalion	LtCol Herbert R. Arney, Jr. (KIA 20 Nov)
	LtCol Walter I. Jordan (to 21 Nov)
	Maj Howard J. Rice
3d Battalion	Maj John F. Shoettel
6th Marines	Col Maurice G. Holmes
1st Battalion	Maj William K. Jones
2d Battalion	LtCol Raymond L. Murray
3d Battalion	LtCol Kenneth F. McLeod
8th Marines	Col Elmer E. Hall
1st Battalion	Maj Lawrence C. Hays, Jr. (WIA 22 Nov)
2d Battalion	Maj Henry P. Crowe
3d Battalion	Maj Robert H. Ruud
10th Marines [artillery]	BGen Thomas R. E. Bourke
1st Battalion	LtCol Presley M. Rixey
2d Battalion	LtCol George R. E. Shell
3d Battalion	LtCol Manly L. Curry
4th Battalion	LtCol Kenneth A. Jorgensen
5th Battalion	Maj Howard V. Hiett
18th Marines [engineer]	Col Cyril W. Martyr
1st Battalion [engineer]	Maj August L. Vogt
2d Battalion [pioneer]	LtCol Chester J. Salazar
3d Battalion [NCB]	Cdr Lawrence E. Tull (USN)
Special & Service Troops, 2d MarDiv	Col Robert C. Thaxton
HQ&S Battalion, 2d MarDiv	LtCol Lyman G. Miller
2d Amphibian Tractor Battalion	Maj Henry C. Drewes (KIA 20 Nov)
	Maj Henry G. Lawrence, Jr. (WIA 20 Nov)
2d Light Tank Battalion	LtCol Alexander B. Swenceski
2d Medical Battalion	LCdr Justin J. Stein (USN)
2d Service Battalion	Col Clarance H. Baldwin
2d Special Weapons Battalion	Maj Guy E. Tannyhill

Half of the 2d Airdrome Battalion arrived from the Ellices on the 24th and was attached to the 2d Defense Battalion. Company D (SCOUT) reconnoitered unoccupied Abaiang, Marakei, and Maiana atolls between November 29 and December 1. LT3/6 arrived at Apamama Atoll on the 26th to garrison it. Tarawa's rebuilt airfield was operational on December 18.

New Britain

Bismarck Archipelago lies 190 miles to the northwest of Bougainville, the northwestern most of the Solomons, and 50 miles off the northeast coast of New Guinea. The principal islands are New Britain (ARABIC) and New Ireland (FOSDICK), both considerably larger than the largest of the Solomons. New Britain is 370 miles long and from 20–60 miles wide. The mountainous terrain, vegetation, and weather are similar to the Solomons, although the weather is hotter and more humid, with rains experienced year around. Administratively the islands were under Australian control as part of the Mandated Territory of New Guinea. Rabaul was the territorial capital.

The Japanese occupied Rabaul in January 1942 and had developed a major naval, air, and army base there by the end of the year. From there the 8th Area Army and Southeastern Area Fleet controlled forces on New Guinea and the South Pacific. Rabaul became the focus of Allied operations in the Southwest Pacific and all operations up to this point had the goal of closing a ring around Rabaul and neutralizing the base. With the 17th and 38th Divisions, 65th Brigade, 6th Air Division, and 11th Air Fleet on the island, the Allies decided to forego a direct assault on Rabaul with the 2d Marine and 3d New Zealand divisions, and instead landed on the island's lightly defended west end.

The Sixth US Army (ALAMO Force) was tasked with Operation DEXTERITY in May 1943 and the 17,850-man 1st MarDiv was assigned to land at Cape Gloucester (DOVETAIL) in Operation BACKHANDER, on December 26. The Division departed Australia between August and October, deploying to staging areas on eastern New Guinea and Goodenough Island where they trained and conducted rehearsals. Aerial bombardment of western New Britain had commenced a month prior to D-Day. Eleven days before the main Marine landing the Army's 112th Cavalry Regiment (Separate) landed at Cape Merkus on the Aeawe Peninsula of New

US landings and Japanese dispositions, New Britain, Bismarck Archipelago, December 1943.

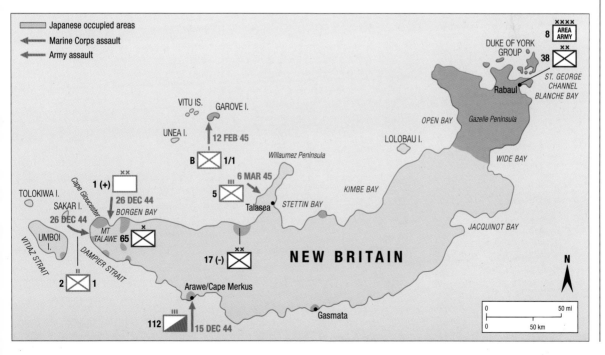

Dense vegetation on New Britain's coast stretched almost unbroken from water's edge all the way up Mt Talawe. The typically small native village shown here in the bottom left, Ulamaingi, sits on the beach west of Cape Gloucester.

Britain's south coast 65 miles west-southwest of Cape Gloucester. The December 14 (Z-Day) landing secured the Peninsula and tied down two Japanese battalions that could have faced the Marines at Cape Gloucester.

The BACKHANDER Attack Force (TF 76) departed its staging areas on December 25 to arrive off Cape Gloucester predawn on December 26 (D-Day). The Japanese detected the convoy en route, but assessed that it was headed to reinforce the Army at Aeawe and prepared to launch massive air attacks there. Off Cape Gloucester the convoy split into the Western and Eastern Attack Groups. The Cape area was defended by the 65th Brigade and 4th Shipping Command, which it had absorbed and collectively known as the Matsuda Force, comprising 10,500 troops.

The Western Attack Force landed the STONEFACE Group, BLT21 (2/1 Marines), at Tauali Village nine miles southwest of the main landing and on the other side of the Cape. The landing occurred at Beach GREEN at 0748 without opposition. These 1,500 troops established a trail block to halt enemy reinforcements from the east. It defeated a single Japanese counterattack on December 30.

The Eastern Attack Group delivered CT C (GREYHOUND Group—7th Marines) on to Beaches YELLOW 1 (BLT37) and 2 (BLT17) on the northwest flank of Borgen Bay six miles to the southeast of the Cape. BLT27, the CT C Reserve, landed on YELLOW 1. This was one of the last landings in which the assault waves were landed by LCVPs rather than amtracs, which were still used as supply carriers. Resistance was finally encountered at 1010 to the west of the beachhead. Japanese air attacks, after vainly attacking Arawe, began that afternoon. Their losses were significant and no further daylight raids occurred. CT B (WILD DUCK Group—1st Marines) landed on YELLOW 1 in the afternoon with BLTs 11 and 31. They moved a short distance to the northwest and established a trail block. There were 11,000 troops ashore by evening. The attack resumed the next morning and was severely hampered by inland swamps much more extensive than thought. CT B pushed west toward the cape and its two airstrips. The Assistant Division Commander (ADC) Group was formed around CT C on December 28. Its mission was to protect the beachhead and halt any Japanese approaching from the east. The ADC Group's staff was provided by assistant 1st MarDiv staff officers. The Division Reserve, CT A—5th Marines—was held at Cape Sudest, New Guinea, and landed late at night on December 28, partly over BLUE, three miles further northwest and nearer to Cape Gloucester, and YELLOW 2. The two airstrips at the Cape were declared secure at noon on December 31. The 1st MarDiv now held a perimeter with a 4.5-mile front and maximum depth of 1.75 miles. The STONEFACE Group (2/1) was withdrawn from Tauali on January 5, 1944 and shuttled by landing craft to Beach BLUE to rejoin the Division on the 12th. A runway was not operational at Airstrip No. 2 until January 31 because of unrelenting rain.

Silimati Point juts out from Cape Gloucester in the background of this photo: beaches YELLOW 1 and 2 are located in the two small bays on the viewer's side of the Point. Target Hill can just be seen in the upper right corner.

1st MarDiv (Reinforced)

Prov Air Liaison Unit, 1st MarDiv (9 x L-4 spotter airplanes)

Combat Team C (Greyhound Group)

7th Marines (BLTs 71, 72, and 73)

1st and 4th Battalions, 11th Marines [artillery]

2d Battalion [pioneer], 17th Marines

Company C, 1st Amphibian Tractor Battalion [LVT(1)]

Company A (Medium), 1st Light Tank Battalion [M4A1]

Company C, 1st Medical Battalion

Company C, 1st MT Battalion

Battery D, 1st Special Weapons Battalion

3d Platoon, Battery A, 1st Special Weapons Battalion

3d Platoon, Company D (Scout), 1st Light Tank Battalion

3d Platoon, 1st MP Company, HQ Battalion, 1st MarDiv

3d Platoon, Ordnance Company, 1st Service Battalion

Detachment, HQ Company, HQ Battalion, 1st MarDiv

Detachment, S&S Company, 1st Service Battalion

Detachment, Special Weapons Group, 12th Defense Battalion

Detachment, Company C, 583d Signal Radar Battalion (USA)

Detachment, 15th Weather Squadron (USAAF)

Detachment, Prov Boat Battalion, 592d Engineer Boat and Shore Regiment (USA)

Combat Team B (Wild Duck Group)

1st Marines (BLTs 22 and 32; - BLT21)

2d Battalion, 11th Marines [artillery]

Detachment, HQ&S Battery, 11th Marines

Company B (-), 1st Amphibian Tractor Battalion [LVT(1)]

Company B (-), 1st Battalion [engineer], 17th Marines

Company D, 1st Medical Battalion

Company A, 1st MT Battalion

Battery C, 1st Special Weapons Battalion

2d Platoon, Battery A, 1st Special Weapons Battalion

1st Platoon, Company D (Scout), 1st Light Tank Battalion

(continued on page 58)

2d Platoon, 1st MP Company, HQ Battalion, 1st MarDiv

2d Platoon, Ordnance Company, 1st Service Battalion

Detachment, S&S Company, 1st Service Battalion

Detachment, Company C, 583d Signal Radar Battalion (USA)

Detachment, Prov Boat Battalion, 592d Engineer Boat and Shore Regiment (USA)*

Battalion Landing Team 21 (Stoneface Group)

2d Battalion, 1st Marines

Battery H, 3d Battalion, 11th Marines

4th Platoon, Battery A, 1st Special Weapons Battalion

2d Platoon, Company B, 1st Amphibian Tractor Battalion [LVT(1)]

1st Platoon (Surgical), Company B, 1st Medical Battalion

37mm AT Gun Platoon, Weapons Company, 1st Marines

Detachment, Company C, 583d Signal Radar Battalion (USA)

Detachment, Prov Boat Battalion, 592d Engineer Boat and Shore Regiment (USA)*

Comprising two LCM(3) and LCVP companies from the Regiment's Boat Battalion and 4.5in. rocket-armed DUKWs of Support Battery (Prov), 2d Engineer Special Bde.

Anti-aircraft Group

Detachment, HQ&S Battery, 12th Defense Battalion

Anti-aircraft Group, 12th Defense Battalion

Detachment, Special Weapons Group, 12th Defense Battalion

one gun section, Seacoast Artillery Group, 12th Defense Battalion

Engineer Group

17th Marines [engineer] (- Companies A, B and C, 1st Battalion; - 2d Battalion)

Cape Gloucester landings and seizure of the airfield, New Britain, December 26, 1943 to December 1, 1944.

(continued on page 59)

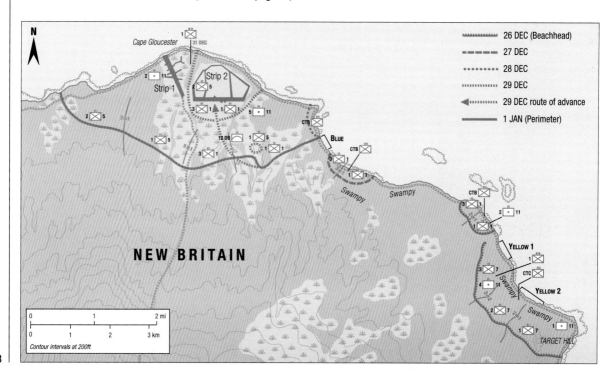

Company E, 1st Medical Battalion

Base Engineer HQ

Reserve Group (CT A)

5th Marines (BLTs 51, 52, and 53)

5th Battalion, 11th Marines [artillery]

Company A, 1st Amphibian Tractor Battalion [LVT(1)/(2)/(A)2]

Company A, 1st Battalion [engineer], 17th Marines

Company C, 1st Light Tank Battalion [M3A1]

Company A, 1st Medical Battalion

Company B, 1st MT Battalion

Battery B, 1st Special Weapons Battalion

1st Platoon, Battery A, 1st Special Weapons Battalion

2d Platoon, Company D (Scout), 1st Light Tank Battalion

1st Platoon, 1st MP Company, HQ Battalion, 1st MarDiv

1st Platoon, Ordnance Company, 1st Service Battalion

Detachment, S&S Company, 1st Service Battalion

Members of the Parish Patrol (a 7th Marines company) embark a landing craft, mechanized Mk III, or LCM(3), en route for Sag Sag, New Britain. The Marine on the far left carries a Thompson M1A1 SMG.

On January 2, the ADC Group, operating semi-independently of the Division, attacked eastward to clear Japanese forces advancing from that direction. This phase consisted of Marine attacks and Japanese counterattacks lasting until January 16. The Japanese then began to withdraw toward Rabaul to reinforce the defenses there rather than continue a futile effort to drive the Americans from western New Britain. Marine patrols would continue to harry the Japanese as they withdrew. A Marine patrol from Cape Gloucester linked up with an Army patrol from Arawe on February 16.

Volupai–Talasea landings and operations, central Willaumez Peninsula, New Britain, March 6–11, 1944.

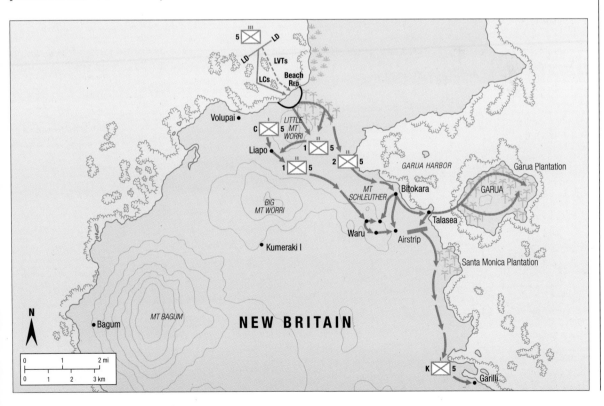

HQ, ADC Group, 1st MarDiv

Attack Group

    7th Marines (- 2d Battalion)

    3d Battalion, 5th Marines

    Company C, 1st Amphibian Tractor Battalion

    3d Platoon, Ordnance Company, 1st Service Battalion

    Detachment, S&S Company, 1st Service Battalion

Artillery Group

    Detachment, HQ and Service Battery, 11th Marines

    1st and 4th Battalions, 11th Marines

Shore Party Group

    HQ Company, 2d Battalion [pioneer], 17th Marines

    Company C, 1st Battalion [engineer], 17th Marines

    Company C, 1st Motor Transport Battalion

    Company C, 1st Medical Battalion

    Company E, 1st Medical Battalion

    Detachment, 1st Service Battalion

Group Reserve

    2d Battalion, 7th Marines

    Battery D (40mm AA), 1st Special Weapons Battalion

    1st Platoon, Company C, 1st Light Tank Battalions

To cut off the withdrawing Japanese the Marines launched Operation APPEASE with the almost 5,000-man Landing Team A, formed on March 1, departing Cape Gloucester on March 5 for the 57-mile trip. It landed at Volupai Plantation midway up the west side of the 35-mile-long Willaumez Peninsula on New Britain's north-central coast. It met only light resistance on Beach RED at 0746 hours on March 6 (D-Day). Most of the withdrawing Japanese were further inland to the south and were not hampered by the Marines, but some elements did unsuccessfully attack. The area was declared secure on the 9th.

Landing Team A, 1st MarDiv

Attack Group

    5th Marines (Reinforced)

    2d Battalion, 11th Marines [artillery]

    Company A [engineer], 17th Marines

    Company F [pioneer], 17th Marines

    Company B (-), 1st Amphibian Tractor Battalion [LVT(1)]

    Company A, 1st Medical Battalion

    Battery B, 1st Special Weapons Battalion

    1st Platoon, Battery A, 1st Special Weapons Battalion

    1st Platoon (+), Company C, 1st Light Tank Battalion [M3A1]

        Platoon, Company A (Medium), 1st Light Tank Battalion [M4A1]

    1st Platoon (-), Company B, 1st MT Battalion

    2d Platoon, Company B, 1st Battalion, 1st Marines [served as MPs]

    Detachment, Ordnance Company, 1st Service Battalion

(continued on page 61)

> Detachment, Graves Registration Section, S&S Company, 1st Service Battalion
>
> Boat Battalion (- Companies B and C), 533d Engineer Boat and Shore Regiment (USA)
>
>> Company A (-), 563d Engineer Boat Maintenance Battalion
>>
>> Detachment, Company F, Shore Battalion, 533d Engineer Boat and Shore Regiment
>>
>> Detachment, Company C, Boat Battalion, 592d Engineer Boat and Shore Regiment
>>
>> Medical Detachment, 533d Engineer Boat and Shore Regiment
>>
>> Prov Division, LCT(5), Flotilla 8, TF 76 (USN)
>
> Reserve Group (not committed)
>
> 1st Battalion (-), 1st Marines
>
> Detachment, Company B, 1st Medical Battalion

The 40th InfDiv began to relieve the 1st MarDiv at Cape Gloucester on April 23 and the last of the Division departed by May 4 to assemble on Pavuvu Island in the Russells to rest and prepare for Peleliu. MacArthur had desired to keep the Division on New Britain, but the Navy feared its amphibious capability would be wasted hunting Japanese remnants. While combat casualties were light compared to other operations, the environment had been extremely difficult for the troops.

Marine Commanders, New Britain	
1st Marine Division	**MajGen William H. Rupertus**
Assistant Division Commander	BGen Lemuel C. Shepherd, Jr. (to 11 Apr)
	BGen Oliver P. Smith
Chief of Staff	Col Amos L. Sims (to 3 Feb)
	Col Oliver P. Smith (to 29 Feb)
	Col John T. Selden
1st Marines	Col William J. Whaling, Jr. (to 29 Feb)
	Col Lewis B. Puller
1st Battalion	LtCol Walker A. Reaves (to 7 Apr)
	Maj Raymond G. Davis
2d Battalion	LtCol James M. Masters, Sr. (to 9 Feb)
	Maj Charles H. Brush, Jr. (to 11 Apr)
	LtCol William W. Stickney
3d Battalion	LtCol Joseph F. Hankins
5th Marines	Col John T. Selden (to 29 Feb)
	Col Oliver P. Smith (to 11 Apr)
	LtCol Henry W. Buse, Jr.
1st Battalion	LtCol William H. Barba
2d Battalion	LtCol Lewis W. Walt (to 5 Jan)
	Maj Gordon D. Gayle
3d Battalion	LtCol David S. McDougal (WIA 7 Jan)
	Maj Joseph S. Skoczylas (WIA 7 Jan)
	LtCol Lewis B. Puller (7–8 Jan)
	LtCol Lewis W. Walt (to 12 Jan)
	LtCol Harold O. Deakin (to 10 Apr)
	Maj Walter McIlhenny

(continued on page 62)

7th Marines	Col Julian N. Frisbie (to 20 Feb)
	Col Herman H. Hannken
1st Battalion	LtCol John E. Weber (to 6 Mar)
	Maj Waite W. Worden (to 11 Apr)
	LtCol Harold O. Deakin
2d Battalion	LtCol Odell M. Conoley (to 7 Feb)
	Maj Charles S. Nichols, Jr. (to 14 Feb)
	LtCol John W. Scott, Jr.
3d Battalion	LtCol William R. Williams (to 3 Jan)
	LtCol Lewis B. Puller (to 8 Jan)
	LtCol Henry W. Bruse, Jr. (to 20 Feb)
	Maj William J. Piper, Jr.
11th Marines [artillery]	Col Robert P. Pepper (to 31 Jan)
	Col William H. Harrison
1st Battalion	LtCol Lewis J. Fields
2d Battalion	LtCol Noah P. Wood, Jr.
3d Battalion	Maj Ernest P. Foley (to 2 Feb)
	LtCol Forest C. Thompson (to 25 Mar)
	LtCol Richard A. Evens
4th Battalion	LtCol Thomas B. Hughes (to 16 Feb)
	LtCol Louis A. Ennis
5th Battalion	LtCol Charles M. Ness
17th Marines [engineer]	Col Harold E. Rosecrans (to 18 Feb)
	Col Francis I. Fenton
1st Battalion [engineer]	LtCol Henry H. Crockett (to 4 Mar)
	Maj John P. McGuinness
2d Battalion [pioneer]	LtCol Levi A. Smith (to 21 Feb)
	Maj Austin S. Igleheart, Jr.
3d Battalion [NC]	Cdr Thomas A. Woods (USN) (to 31 Jan)
	LtCdr James T. Redd (USN)
Service Troops, 1st MarDiv	LtCol Herman H. Hanneken (to 20 Feb then vacant)
HQ&S Battalion, 1st MarDiv	LtCol Frank R. Worthington
1st Amphibian Tractor Battalion	Maj Francis H. Cooper
1st Light Tank Battalion	LtCol Charles G. Meints (to 15 Apr)
	Maj Donald J. Robinson
1st Medical Battalion	Cdr Everett B. Keck (USN) (to 27 Feb)
	Cdr Stanley P. Wallin (USN) (to 18 Apr)
	Cdr Emil E. Napp (USN)
1st Motor Transport Battalion	Maj Kimber H. Boyer
1st Service Battalion	LtCol Edward F. Doyle
1st Special Weapons Battalion	Maj Raymond G. Davis (to 5 Apr)
	Maj John P. Leonard, Jr.
12th Defense Battalion	Col William H. Harrison (to 31 Jan)
	LtCol Merlyn D. Holmes

Roi-Namur

The Marshall, Caroline, and Mariana Islands comprised the Japanese Mandated Territory, taken from Germany in 1914 and granted to Japan by the League of Nations in 1920. Japan developed air and naval bases on the islands from the 1930s. The governing South Seas Bureau was headquartered in the Palaus and the 4th Fleet, responsible for the defense of the Mandates, was headquartered on Truk Atoll (pronounced "Chuck") in the Carolines. A major naval base, Truk was described as "Japan's Pearl Harbor."

The Allies' first thrust into the Mandates was aimed at Kwajalein Atoll (CARILLON) in the Marshalls. It would be the first assault on actual Japanese territory and was assigned to VAC. The world's largest atoll is 66 miles long and 18 miles wide with 93 islands and islets. It was an outlying bastion for the Marshalls' main defended atoll, Jaluit, 245 miles to the southeast. The Gilberts are some 500 miles to the south and Pearl Harbor is 2,440 miles west. The 4th MarDiv was assigned the double islands of Roi-Namur (BURLESQUE-CAMOUFLAGE) on the north-central rim of the atoll. The Army's 7th InfDiv would take Kwajalein Island (PORCELAIN) on February 1–4 on the atoll's south end, 44 miles southeast of Roi-Namur.

Roi and Namur are connected by a sandspit and a 500yd-long concrete causeway. Roi is 1,170 by 1,250yds and Namur is 800 by 890yds. Both sand islands are only a few feet above sea level. Roi, cleared of vegetation, was occupied by a figure-of-four-shaped airfield while Namur was crowded with barracks, shops, and support facilities and palms. They were defended by 3,563 men of the 61st Guard Force Dispatched Force, 24th Air Flotilla HQ, aircraft service personnel, and laborers.

Roi-Namur, Phase I, D-Day January 31, 1944: securing adjacent islands.

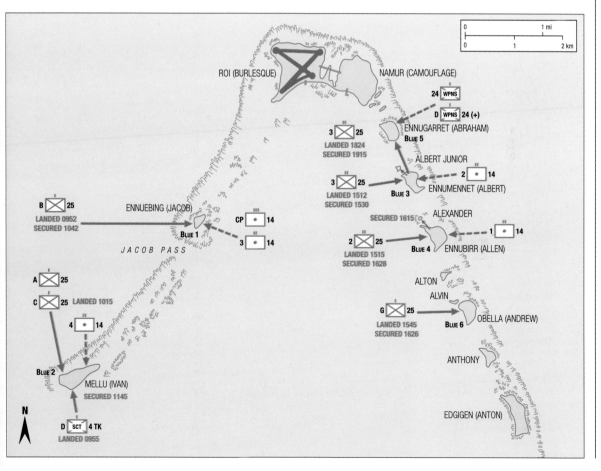

The Division arrived at Kwajalein aboard Northern Attack Force (TF 53) in the early hours of January 31 (D-Day). It began an operation under BGen Underhill securing adjacent islets to the southwest and southeast of Roi-Namur, termed Operation FLINTLOCK Phase I. The map on page 63 depicts which units landed where, their code names, actual landing times, and when they were declared secure. Once secure, 3/14 (75mm) and 4/14 (105mm) set up on Ennuebing and Mellu respectively, while 1/14 and 2/14 (both 75mm) were established on Ennubirr and Ennumennet respectively, to support the next day's landing on Roi Namur. The 14th Marines' CP was on Ennuebing. On Ennugarret, 400yds southeast of Namur, the 24th Marines emplaced five 75mm SPMs, seventeen 37mm AT guns, four 81mm and nine 60mm mortars, and 61 machine guns to support the D+1 landing.

Regimental Combat Team 25 (IVAN Landing Group)
25th Marines (Reinforced)
14th Marines [artillery]
1st Composite Engineer Battalion
10th Amphibian Tractor Battalion (Reinforced) [110 x LVT(2)]
Company A, 11th Amphibian Tractor Battalion [30 x LVT(2)]
Prov LVT(2) Platoon, 1st Armored Amphibian Tractor Battalion [14 x LVT(2)]
Company B, 1st Armored Amphibian Tractor Battalion [LVT(A)1]
Company D, 1st Armored Amphibian Tractor Battalion [LVT(A)1]
Company A, 4th Light Tank Battalion [M5A1]
Company D (Scout), 4th Light Tank Battalion
Battery B, 4th Special Weapons Battalion
Company A, 4th Medical Battalion
Company A, 4th MT Battalion
1st Platoon, Battery A, 4th Special Weapons Battalion
1st Platoon, 4th MP Company
1st Platoon, S&S Company, 4th Service Battalion
1st Platoon, Ordnance Company, 4th Service Battalion
Detachment, 1st Joint Assault Signal Company
Detachment, HQ Company, HQ Battalion, 4th MarDiv
Detachment, Signal Company, HQ Battalion, 4th MarDiv
Band Section

The Roi Island airfield being pounded by a carrier air strike just prior to D-Day. The causeway connecting Namur is to the left. The improved precision of air strikes and naval gunfire, together with a more effective selection of ordnance, meant that a large percentage of the defenders were killed prior to the assault, something that had not occurred on Tarawa.

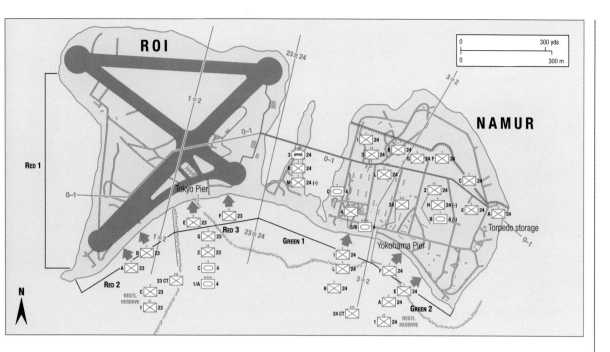

Roi-Namur: Phase II, D+1 February 1–2, 1944.

Marine casualties were fewer than two dozen, but the operation was hampered by rough seas and amtrac assembly delays. The Japanese lost 35 men with five prisoners taken. IVAN Landing Group was dissolved at 0700 hours, February 1 and reassigned as the Division Reserve for Phase II.

Phase II commenced on D+1 with the planned W-Hour at 1000. Roi-Namur was being heavily pounded by naval gunfire, artillery, and from the air. Again there were delays in launching the landing force and it was found that the 10th Amtrac Battalion was short 48 LVTs because of breakdowns, stranded, and scattered amtracs supporting RCT25. Some RCT24 rear waves were boated in LCVPs. The order to attack was given over an hour behind schedule.

RCT23 hit Beaches RED 2 (1/23) and RED 3 (2/23) on the south coast of Roi at 1157 and swept toward the airfield. They pushed across the island against light resistance, reaching the north shore at 1800 and 1700, respectively. The aggressive use of medium tanks, which failed to pause at the O-1 Line on the north side of the main runway, turned into a general rush to the north shore with amphibian tanks joining in and the infantry hard-pressed to keep up. The reserve 3/23 was ashore by 1500, but only conducted mop up. Roi was declared secure at 1802.

Namur, covered with vegetation and large numbers of buildings, proved a more difficult objective. RCT24 came ashore at 1155 on GREEN 1 (3/24), which included the connecting sandspit and causeway, and GREEN 2 (2/24). As insufficient LVTs were available for the two assault battalions' reserve companies, a last-minute decision was made to land Companies A and B/1/24 (Regimental Reserve), attached to 2/24 and 3/24. Anti-tank ditches, trenches, and rubble halted the armored amtracs leading the troop amtracs ashore. At 1305, Marine satchel charges thrown unknowingly into a torpedo storage bunker detonated the warheads and two munitions magazines resulting in 20 dead and 100 wounded in companies E and F, half the casualties suffered by 2/24 on Namur. Company A was attached to 2/24 to allow it to continue its mission. The O-1 Line, 300yds north of the beaches, was gained within two hours, but the assault units became intermingled. Resistance grew heavier and dense vegetation and debris slowed the advance north. The Marines dug in for the night just north of the O-1 Line with seven companies on-line. The advance continued at 0900 and the northernmost point of Namur was reached at 1215. The island was declared secure at 1418. Only 91 Japanese prisoners were taken on both islands.

Marines of the 23d Marines on Roi pause momentarily to watch the mushroom cloud over Namur after a torpedo warehouse was unknowingly detonated.

4th MarDiv (Reinforced)

Regimental Combat Team 23 (Roi)

    23d Marines (Reinforced)

    3d Composite Engineer Battalion

    4th Amphibian Tractor Battalion [100 x LVT(2)]

    Companies A and C, 1st Armored Amphibian Tractor Battalion [LVT(A)1]

    Company C (Medium), 4th Light Tank Battalion [M4A2]

        1st Platoon, Company A, 4th Light Tank Battalion [M5A1]

    Company C, 4th Medical Battalion

    Company C, 4th MT Battalion

    Battery C, 4th Special Weapons Battalion

    3d Platoon, 4th MP Company

    3d Platoon, Battery A, 4th Special Weapons Battalion

    Detachment, 1st Joint Assault Signal Company

    Band Section

Regimental Combat Team 24 (Namur)

    24th Marines (Reinforced)

    2d Composite Engineer Battalion

    10th Amphibian Tractor Battalion (LVT[2])*

    Companies B and D, 1st Armored Amphibian Tractor Battalion [LVT(A)1]*

    Company B, 4th Light Tank Battalion [M5A1]

    Company B, 4th Medical Battalion

    Company B, 4th MT Battalion

    Battery D, 4th Special Weapons Battalion

    2d Platoon, 4th MP Company

    2d Platoon, Battery A, 4th Special Weapons Battalion

    Detachment, 1st Joint Assault Signal Company

    Band Section

    Transferred from RCT25.

Regimental Combat Team 25 (Division Reserve)

    25th Marines (Reinforced)

    1st Composite Engineer Battalion

    Company A, 11th Amphibian Tractor Battalion [LVT(2)]

        Prov LVT(2) Platoon, 1st Armored Amphibian Tractor Battalion

    Company A (-), 4th Light Tank Battalion [M5A1]

    Company D (Scout), 4th Light Tank Battalion

    Company A, 4th Medical Battalion

    Company A, 4th MT Battalion

    Battery B, 4th Special Weapons Battalion

    1st Platoon, Battery A, 4th Special Weapons Battalion

    1st Platoon, 4th MP Company

    1st Platoon, Ordnance Company, 4th Service Battalion

    1st Platoon, S&S Company, 4th Service Battalion

(continued on page 67)

Detachment, 1st Joint Assault Signal Company

Band Section

Support Group

HQ Battalion, 4th MarDiv (-)

20th Marines (-)

1st Armored Amphibian Tractor Battalion (-)

4th Light Tank Battalion (-)

4th Medical Battalion (-)

4th MT Battalion (-)

4th Service Battalion (-)

4th Special Weapons Battalion (-)

15th Defense Battalion (Garrison Force)

A Japanese sailor surrenders on Namur after emerging from a massive, concrete, steel-doored bunker. He was one of 91 prisoners taken on the twin islands.

RCT25 went on to clear 47, mostly unoccupied, Kwajalein Atoll islets between February 2 and 5 (Phases III–V). In a related operation BLT 106-2, VAC Reconnaissance Company, and 1st Defense Battalion (SUNDANCE Landing Force) secured Majuro Atoll to the southwest of Kwajalein between January 30 and February 1.

The 4th MarDiv had assembled on Maui, TH by the end of February and began to prepare for the Marianas. The airfield on Roi was refurbished and used to bomb by-passed Japanese islands in the Marshalls to the end of the war.

Marine Commanders, Roi-Namur	
V Amphibious Corps	**MajGen Holland M. Smith**
Chief of Staff	BGen Graves B. Erskine
VAC HQ&S Battalion	Maj Thomas R. Wert
VAC Signal Battalion	LtCol James H. N. Hudnall
1st Armored Amphibian Tractor Battalion	Maj Louis Metzger
4th Amphibian Tractor Battalion	LtCol Colvis C. Coffman
10th Amphibian Tractor Battalion	Maj Victor J. Croizat
1st Defense Battalion	Col Louis A. Hohn
15th Defense Battalion	LtCol Francis B. Loomis, Jr.

4th Marine Division	MajGen Harry Schmidt
Assistant Division Commander	BGen James L. Underhill
Chief of Staff	Col William W. Rogers
14th Marines [artillery]	Col Louis G. DeHaven
1st Battalion	LtCol Harry J. Zimmer
2d Battalion	LtCol George B. Wilson, Jr.
3d Battalion	LtCol Robert E. MacFarlane
4th Battalion	Maj Carl A. Youngdale
20th Marines [engineer]	Col Lucian W. Burnham
1st Battalion [engineer]	Maj Richard G. Ruby
2d Battalion [pioneer]	LtCol Otto Lessing
3d Battalion [NCB]	LCdr William G. Byrne (USN)
23d Marines	Col Louis R. Jones
1st Battalion	LtCol Franklin A. Hart
2d Battalion	LtCol Edward J. Dillon
3d Battalion	LtCol John J. Cosgrove, Jr.
24th Marines	Col Franklin A. Hart
1st Battalion	LtCol Aquilla J. Dyess (KIA 2 Feb)
	Maj Maynard C. Schultz
2d Battalion	LtCol Francis H. Brink (WIA 1 Feb)
3d Battalion	LtCol Austin R. Brunelli
25th Marines	Col Samuel C. Cumming
1st Battalion	LtCol Clarence J. O'Donnell
2d Battalion	LtCol Lewis C. Hudson, Jr.
3d Battalion	LtCol Justice M. Chambers
Special & Service Troops, 4th MarDiv	Col Emmett W. Skinner
HQ&S Battalion, 4th MarDiv	LtCol Melvin L. Krulewitch
4th Light Tank Battalion	Maj Richard K. Schmidt
4th Medical Battalion	LCdr Stewart W. Shimonek (USN)
4th MT Battalion	LtCol Ralph L. Schiesswohl
4th Service Battalion	Maj John L. Lamprey, Jr.
4th Special Weapons Battalion	LtCol Alexander A. Vandegrift

Eniwetok

Eniwetok (or Brown) Atoll (DOWNSIDE) is 337 miles northwest of Kwajalein and served as an out-guard to Truk some 400 miles to the southwest. The roughly circular atoll is 21 miles across northwest to southeast and 17 miles from northeast to southwest. It has 30 islets, on three of which the Japanese established defenses: Eniwetok (or Brown) Island (PRIVILEGE, 0.25 miles wide, 2 miles long); on the atoll's southeast rim, Parry (HEARTSTRINGS, 600yds wide, 2 miles long) 2.5 miles northeast of Eniwetok; and Engebi (FRAGILE, 1,500 x 2,000 x 2,100yds) on the north rim. In mid-1943 an airstrip was built on triangular-shaped Engebi. The islands are low and flat, covered with brush and palms. They were defended by 2,586 troops of the 1st Amphibious Brigade, 59 from the 61st Defense Force (coast defense guns), and some 850 construction troops, stranded sailors, air service personnel, and laborers.

It was originally planned to seize Eniwetok on March 19, 1944 with the 2d MarDiv, and the 27th InfDiv would take Kusaie to the southeast at the end of the month. A later plan called for the 3d MarDiv to secure Eniwetok after completing the New Ireland operation in April. Instead it was decided to take Eniwetok soon after securing Kwajalein. Recently formed Tactical Group 1, VAC was given the task, having served as the Fleet Reserve at Kwajalein. It contained 5,820 Marines and sailors, and 4,556 soldiers, totaling 10,376. D-Day was set for February 17 and the group departed aboard the Eniwetok Expeditionary Group (TG 51.11). Carrier strikes had been conducted on the atoll since the end of January.

D-Day Adjacent Islands (Phase I)—VAC Reconnaissance Company secured unoccupied Aitsu and Rujiyoru southeast of Engebi by 1400. The 2d Separate Pack Howitzer and 104th Field Artillery Battalions landed on these islands, respectively, to support the Engebi assault. Company D (Scout), 4th Tank Battalion secured Elugelab, Bogon, and other islets west of Engebi in the early morning of D+1 to prevent the enemy escaping from Engebi.

D+1 Engebi (Phase II)—The landings were on the island's southwest shore with 2/22 coming ashore on Beach BLUE 3 as 1/22 landed on WHITE 1 at W-Hour, 0845, to be followed by 3/22 (Regimental Reserve). Tank Company, 22d Marines and a platoon of Cannon Company, 106th Infantry followed ashore. The island was secured at 0800, February 19.

D+2 Eniwetok (Phase III)—The Y-Hour 0918 landing was on the island's northwest shore with BLT106-3 landing on YELLOW 1. BLT106-1 landed on YELLOW 1 and was followed by the Tank Company, 22d Marines; a platoon of Cannon Company, 106th Infantry; and 3/22 (Regimental Reserve). It was secured at 1420, February 19 by the Army, but this took longer than expected.

D+4 Parry (Phase III)—The February 21 landings were on the island's west side at Z-Hour, 0900. The 2/2 landed on GREEN 2 followed by 3/22. The 1/22 landed on GREEN 3. Tank Company, 22d Marines; Company D (Scout), 4th Tank Battalion; and VAC Reconnaissance Company joined the attack in the afternoon. BLT106-3 was the floating reserve. Parry was secured at 0930 the next day.

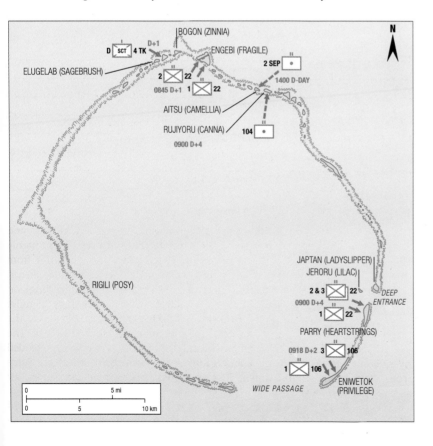

Eniwetok Atoll, February 17–23, 1944.

Assault troops of the 22d Marines wade ashore on one of Eniwetok Atoll's small, undefended islands, February 1944. Wading across fringing coral reefs was a slow and difficult undertaking due to the uneven bottom, potholes, outcroppings, currents, and surf surges. Upon reaching the beach, the Marines would rush to the nearest cover and concealment.

All three landings were led by Company A, 708th Amphibian Tank Battalion. The 10th Defense Battalion, the garrison force, served as the Group Reserve, forming a 500-man provisional battalion of five companies, but it was not needed.

While these operations were underway, Company D (Scout), 4th Tank Battalion secured eight islets on Eniwetok's western rim from February 18 to 20; only Rigilli was defended by a squad. VAC Reconnaissance Company secured ten unoccupied islets on the atoll's eastern rim on the 19th, then secured Japtan (LADYSLIPPER) north of Parry. The 2d Separate Pack Howitzer Battalion then landed to support the Parry D+4 assault.

The atoll was secured with the Marines losing 276 dead and missing and 568 wounded, the Army 94 dead and 311 wounded. Only 74 Japanese prisoners were taken. The 106th Infantry was detached from Tactical Group 1 and garrisoned the atoll with 3d Army Defense Battalion. The 22d Marines garrisoned Kwajalein. Between March 7 and April 5, 1944 it secured 14 unoccupied atolls and islands in the Lesser Marshalls as part of Operation FLINTLOCK JR. Three airfields were built in Eniwetok and supported the Marianas operation to the north.

Tactical Group 1, VAC

HQ, Tactical Group 1, VAC

    708th Prov Amphibian Tractor Battalion (-) [102 x LVT(2) + 17 spares] (USA)*

        Company A, 708th Amphibian Tank Battalion [17 x LVT(A)1] (USA)

    VAC Amphibious Reconnaissance Company

    Company D (Scout), 4th Light Tank Battalion

    Portable Surgical Hospital No. 1 (Prov)

    Shore Party

Formed from 708th Amphibian Tank Battalion with four company-size groups of 32 x LVT(2)s each.

22d Marines (Reinforced)

    2d Separate Pack Howitzer Battalion

    Engineer Company, 22d Marines

    Medical Company, 22d Marines

    MT Company, 22d Marines

    Tank Company, 22d Marines [M4A1]

    Groups B and C, 708th Prov Amphibian Tractor Battalion (USA)

    Parties, 2d Joint Assault Signal Company

(continued on page 71)

106th Infantry Regiment (Reinforced) (- 2d Battalion) (USA)

    104th Field Artillery Battalion (105mm Howitzer)

    104th Engineer Combat Battalion (Corps) (- one company)

        Company B (-), 102d Engineer Combat Battalion

    Company C, 766th Tank Battalion [M4A1]

    Group D, 708th Prov Amphibian Tractor Battalion

    Companies C and D (-), 102d Medical Battalion

    Prov DUKW Battery, 7th InfDiv Artillery [30 x DUKW, 4 x LVT(2)]

    Detachment, 295th Joint Assault Signal Company

    Parties, 2d Joint Assault Signal Company (USMC)

Group Reserve

    10th Defense Battalion

Marine and Army Commanders, Eniwetok	
Tactical Group 1, VAC	**BGen Thomas E. Watson**
22d Marines (Reinforced)	Col John T. Walker
1st Battalion	LtCol Walfried H. Fromhold
2d Battalion	LtCol Donn C. Hart
3d Battalion	Maj Clair W. Shisler
2d Separate Pack Howitzer Battalion	LtCol Edwin C. Ferguson (to 17 Feb)
	Maj Alfred M. Mahoney
106th Infantry Regt (-) (Reinforced)	Col Russell G. Ayers
1st Battalion	LtCol Winslow Cornett
3d Battalion	LtCol Harold J. Mizony
104th Field Artillery Battalion	LtCol Van Nostrand
104th Engineer Combat Battalion	LtCol John R. Sharp
3d Army Defense Battalion	LtCol Ralph W. Oakley
10th Defense Battalion	LtCol Wallace O. Thompson
708th Prov Amphibian Tractor Battalion	Maj James L. Rogers

Saipan

The string of the Marianas (GATEWAY) is 3,400 miles west of Pearl Harbor; Eniwetok is 1,300 miles east, and Tokyo is 1,260 miles northwest. The 425-mile-long chain has 15 hilly, volcanic islands, all of which were Japanese territory with the exception of Guam on the south end. The American possession had been seized by Japan in December 1941.

Saipan (TATTERSALLS), near the southern end of the chain and the Japanese administrative center, was the first objective of Operation FORAGER. Saipan measures 5.5 by 12.5 miles and has an elevation of 1,554ft, making it the second largest of the Marianas. Much of the island was planted with sugarcane and the rest covered by scrub trees, brush, and high grass. The Japanese had built airfields on both ends of the island. Tinian is three miles to the south and Guam 100 miles to the southwest.

The US landing forces were under the control of LtGen Holland Smith, commanding the Expeditionary Troops (TF 58) discussed in the FMFPac section

Japanese dispositions, Southern Marianas, June 1944.

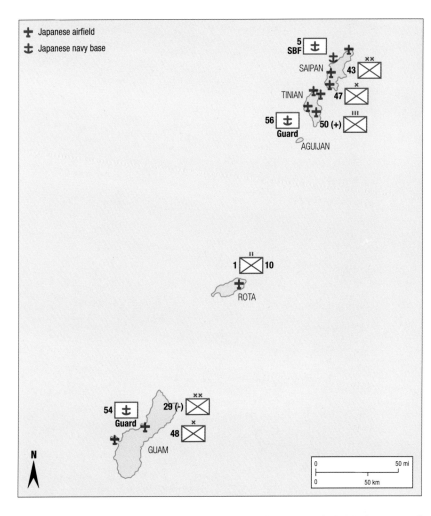

on pages 10–11. The Northern Troops and Landing Force (TG 56.1) consisted of VAC, an Army and two Marine divisions, totaling 66,779 troops of whom 47,510 were Marines. This was not only the Marines' first two-division landing, but the first of the Pacific War. The Army's XXIV Corps Artillery was attached to VAC and VAC Artillery to XXIV Corps. This was due to previous positioning for the cancelled Yap operation. The 1st Prov MarBde was the VAC floating reserve until released for the Guam assault on June 15. The 77th InfDiv was the General Reserve in Hawaii.

A number of new weapons and innovations were introduced on Saipan. Extensive use was made of rocket-firing LCI(G)s to cover the landing. Napalm bombs were used for the first time in the Pacific as were A-H1B flameguns mounted in M3A1 tanks and the 4.5in. rocket detachments. A third of the 719 amtracs employed were the new LVT(4)s. Extensive use was made of Army amphibian tractor and artillery battalions as well as other attached Army units. It was proposed that the LVTs carry the assault troops up to a mile inland to their objectives. This was rejected by the 2d MarDiv because of difficult terrain, but the 4th MarDiv attempted it with limited success.

After completing rehearsals, VAC departed Hawaii between May 25 and 30. The 43d Division, 47th Independent Mixed Brigade, and 5th Special Base Force—31,700 troops, most of who had arrived on Saipan earlier that same month—rushed to prepare defenses. The Force arrived off of Saipan on D-Day morning, June 15. Battleships had been pounding the island since D-2 and air raids had been hitting it for over a month.

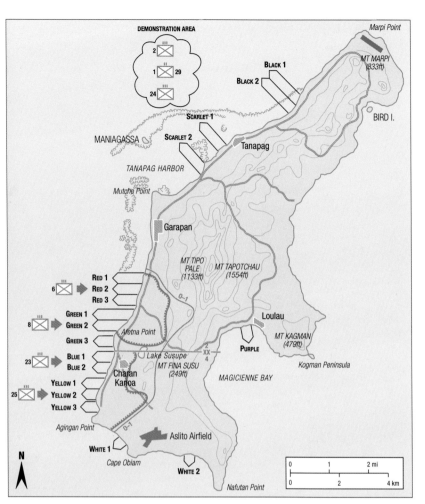

Saipan, D-Day, June 15, 1944.

V Amphibious Corps (Northern Troops and Landing Force) (2,296)
VAC HQ&S Battalion (-)
VAC Amphibious Reconnaissance Battalion (- Company A)
VAC Medical Battalion (-)
VAC Signal Battalion (-)
VAC MT Company (-)
VAC Prov LVT Group (-)
VAC Prov Engineer Group (-)
2d Separate Engineer Battalion
7th Field Depot (Reinforced) (-)
3d Marine Ammunition Company
18th, 19th, and 20th Marine Depot Companies
31st Medical Field Hospital (USA)
2d and 3d Prov Portable Surgical Hospitals (USA)
Air Warning Squadron (Air Transportable) 5 (-)*
Detachments, 680th, 726th, and 763d Aircraft Warning Signal Companies (USAAF)

(continued on page 74)

Detachment, Company C, 101st Signal Battalion, Separate (USA)

Redesignated Assault Air Warning Squadron 5 on July 10.

XXIV Corps Artillery (USA) (2,682)
420th Field Artillery Group (USA)
2d Battalion, 55th Coast Artillery Regiment (155mm Gun) (Mobile)
32d Coast Artillery Gun Battalion (155mm Gun)
145th Field Artillery Battalion (155mm Howitzer)
225th Field Artillery Battalion (155mm Howitzer)
477th Transportation Corps Amphibious Truck Company (Colored)
Prov AAA Group (USA) (949)
751st AAA Gun Battalion (90mm) (-)
864th AAA Automatic Weapons Battalion (40mm/.50cal) (-)
1st Battalion, 2d Marines (Reinforced) (Eastern Landing Group) (1,084)
Company A, VAC Amphibious Reconnaissance Battalion

While much of Saipan's inland terrain was comparatively flat, making movement on foot easy, the area around Lake Susupe behind Charan Kanoa was swampy and more restrictive than thought. The rough inland terrain also halted amtracs attempting to reach the O-1 Line behind the town.

On D-1 the 2d and 4th MarDiv's reserve regiments, 2d and 24th Marines, and 1/29 conducted a demonstration off the northwest coast. It failed to convince the Japanese that the landing would occur there, but it prevented them from shifting troops south. 1/2 was tasked with a VAC special landing operation on the east coast near Laulau (Beach PURPLE) on 14/15 June to seize central Mt Tapotchau and await relief. It was canceled for fear of it being cut off. H-Hour was 0830, but was postponed by ten minutes.

Four air liaison teams and four shore fire-control parties, 2d Joint Assault Signal Company were attached to each CT. A seven-man team was attached to each division and RCT from Mobile Communications Unit No. 18, Group Pacific 6 (USN) for back-up communications. Most battalion's beaches were 600yds wide.

2d MarDiv (Reinforced) (21,746)
Combat Team 2 (Division Reserve)
2d Marines (Reinforced) (- 1st Battalion)
Company A (-), 1st Battalion [engineer], 18th Marines
Company E (-), 2d Medical Battalion
Detachment (Bomb Disposal Squad), HQ Company, 1st Battalion [engineer], 18th Marines
1st Band Section (-)
Combat Team 6
6th Marines (Reinforced)
2d Amphibian Tractor Battalion [LVT(2)/(4)]
Detachment, 5th Amphibian Tractor Battalion [LVT(4)]
Company B, 1st Battalion [engineer], 18th Marines
Company D, 2d Medical Battalion
Company A (+ 3d Platoon, Company C), 2d Tank Battalion [M4A2]

(continued on page 75)

3d Platoon, Company D (Flamethrower), 2d Tank Battalion [M3A1/M5A1]

2d Prov Rocket Detachment (-)

Detachment (Bomb Disposal Squad), HQ Company, 1st Battalion [engineer], 18th Marines

2d Band Section

Combat Team 8

8th Marines (Reinforced)

715th Amphibian Tractor Battalion [LVT(2)/(4)] (USA)

Company C, 1st Battalion [engineer], 18th Marines

Company C, 2d Medical Battalion

Company A (+ 2d Platoon, Company C), 2d Tank Battalion [M4A2]

    2d Platoon, Company D (Flamethrower), 2d Tank Battalion [M3A1/M5A1]

Detachment, 2d Prov Rocket Detachment

Detachment (Bomb Disposal Squad), HQ Company, 1st Battalion [engineer], 18th Marines

3d Band Section

Division Reserve

1st Battalion, 29th Infantry (Reinforced)

1st Platoon (AT), Weapons Company, 2d Marines

1st Platoon, Company A, 1st Battalion [engineer], 18th Marines

Detachment, 1st Band Section

Division Artillery

10th Marines (artillery)

2d 155mm Howitzer Battalion, VAC

Detachment, 1st Marine Amphibian Truck Company

Detachment, 5th Amphibian Tractor Battalion (LVT[4])

Marine Observation Squadron 2

2d Armored Amphibian Tractor Battalion (LVT[A]4)

Support Group

HQ&S Company, 18th Marines [engineer]

HQ Company, 1st Battalion [engineer], 18th Marines

HQ Battalion, 2d MarDiv

    HQ, Signal, MP, and Reconnaissance Companies

2d Medical Battalion

    HQ&S Company, Company B

2d Tank Battalion

    HQ&S Company, Company C (-), Company D (-)

2d Service Battalion

    HQ, S&S, and Ordnance Companies

5th Amphibian Tractor Battalion (-) [LVT(4)]

18th NC Battalion

2d Joint Assault Signal Company (-)

Detachment, 7th Field Depot

3d Platoon, 604th Quartermaster Graves Registration Company (USA)

Detachment, Air Warning Squadron (Air Transportable) 5

Shore Party

The 2dMarDiv landed on the west coast at 0843, south of Garapan, the administrative center. Its beaches were north of Charan Kanoa with the 4th MarDiv to its south. An unexpected current, inability of control vessels to accompany the LVTs across the reef, and enemy fire caused battalions to land north of their assigned beaches. 2/6 and 3/6 landed on Beaches RED 1 and 2 rather than 2 and 3. 2/8 and 3/8 both landed on GREEN 1 rather than 1 and 2. 1/29 came ashore on GREEN 2 at 1450 and was attached to CT8. The 2d MarDiv made the most headway on D-Day, pushing almost halfway across the island, but it did not achieve its O-1 Line. CT2 (-) landed piecemeal on D+1. 1/2, its special mission canceled, had landed on BLUE 1 at 1800 and rejoined its parent regiment. 2/2 was attached to the CT6 and 2/6 to CT2 as it was wedged into position between CTs 2 and 8. 3/2 had landed on D-Day as a reserve. 3/10 and 4/10, the 105mm battalions, came ashore on GREEN 3 on D+1.

4th MarDiv (Reinforced) (21,618)

Regimental Landing Team 23

    23d Marines (Reinforced)

    10th Amphibian Tractor Battalion (-) [LVT(2)]

        Company C, 11th Amphibian Tractor Battalion [LVT(2)]

        Company B, 534th Amphibian Tractor Battalion (+ detachment, Company C) [LVT(2)/(4)] (USA)

    708th Amphibian Tank Battalion (- Companies C and D) [LVT(A)1/(A)4] (USA)

    121st NC Battalion (+)

    Company C, 1st Battalion [engineer], 20th Marines

    Company C, 4th Medical Battalion

    Company C, 4th MT Battalion

    Company B, 4th Tank Battalion [M4A2]

    Company C, 4th Tank Battalion [M4A2]

    Company D (Flamethrower) (-), 4th Tank Battalion [M3A1/M5A1]

    311th Transportation Corps Port Company (Colored) (USA)

    3d Platoon, 4th MP Company

    3d Platoon, Ordnance Company, HQ Battalion, 4th MarDiv

    3d Platoon, S&S Company, HQ Battalion, 4th MarDiv

    Detachment, 1st Joint Assault Signal Company

    Detachment, 7th Field Depot

    3d Band Section

Regimental Landing Team 25

    25th Marines (Reinforced)

    773d Amphibian Tractor Battalion (USA) [LVT(2)]

        Company C, 534th Amphibian Tractor Battalion (USA) (-) [LVT(2)/(4)]

    Company C, 708th Amphibian Tank Battalion (USA) [LVT(A)1]

    Company D, 708th Amphibian Tank Battalion (USA) [LVT(A)1]

    2d Battalion [pioneer], 20th Marines

    Company A, 1st Battalion [engineer], 20th Marines

    Company A, 4th Medical Battalion

(continued on page 78)

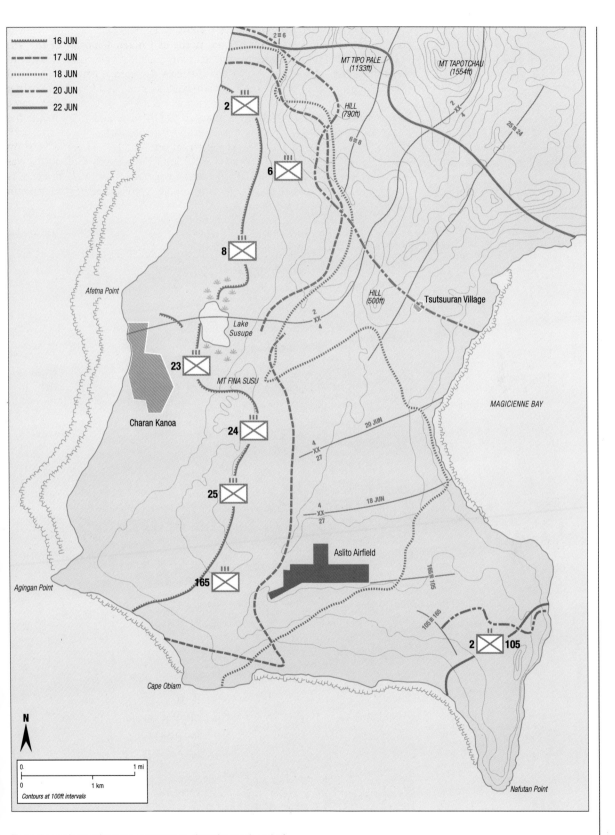

Key:
- 16 JUN
- 17 JUN
- 18 JUN
- 20 JUN
- 22 JUN

MT TIPO PALE (1133ft)

MT TAPOTCHAU (1554ft)

2 ≡ 6

2

HILL (790ft)

6

6 ≡ 8

2 XX 4

25 ≡ 24

8

Afetna Point

Lake Susupe

HILL (500ft)

Tsutsuuran Village

2 XX 4

23

MT FINA SUSU

Charan Kanoa

MAGICIENNE BAY

24

20 JUN

4 XX 27

25

4 XX 27

18 JUN

Agingan Point

165

Aslito Airfield

165 ≡ 105

105 ≡ 165

2   105

Cape Obiam

N

0.   1 mi

0   1 km

Contours at 100ft intervals

Nafutan Point

Tactical complexity: the joint operation to clear the south end of
Saipan while continuing the advance north, June 16–22, 1944.

Though the Charan Kanoa sugar mill, in Saipan's second largest town, was heavily damaged by naval gunfire, the still-standing smoke stack sheltered a Japanese artillery forward observer for several days after the landing.

Company A, 4th MT Battalion

Company A, 4th Tank Battalion [M4A2]

    1st Platoon, Company D (Flamethrower), 4th Tank Battalion [M3A1/M5A1]

539th Transportation Corps Port Company (Colored) (USA)

1st Platoon, 4th MP Company

1st Platoon, Ordnance Company, HQ Battalion, 4th MarDiv

1st Platoon, S&S Company, HQ Battalion, 4th MarDiv

Detachment, 1st Joint Assault Signal Company

Detachment, 7th Field Depot

1st Band Section

Regimental Landing Team 24 (Division Reserve)

24th Marines (Reinforced)

Company B, 1st Battalion [engineer], 20th Marines

Company B, 4th Medical Battalion

Company B, 4th MT Battalion

539th Transportation Corps Port Company (Colored) (USA)

2d Platoon, 4th MP Company

2d Platoon, Ordnance Company, HQ Battalion, 4th MarDiv

2d Platoon, S&S Company, HQ Battalion, 4th MarDiv

Detachment, 1st Joint Assault Signal Company

2d Band Section

Division Artillery

14th Marines (artillery)

4th 105mm Artillery Battalion, VAC*

2d Marine Amphibian Truck Company

1st Platoon, Company A, 534th Amphibian Tractor Battalion [LVT(4)] (USA)

Referred to as 5/14 Marines in contemporary reports as this was its original designation.

Division Engineers

20th Marines [engineer] (-)

HQ, 7th Field Depot

Support Group

HQ Battalion (-), 4th MarDiv

4th Medical Battalion (-)

4th MT Battalion (-)

4th Tank Battalion (-)

4th Service Battalion (-)

534th Amphibian Tractor Battalion (-) (USA)

4th Reconnaissance Company

Marine Observation Squadron 4

1st Joint Assault Signal Company (-)

1st Prov Rocket Detachment

Detachment, Air Warning Squadron (Air Transportable) 5

The 4th MarDiv landed at 0840 on the lower south coast with the 2d MarDiv to its north. 3/23 and 2/23 landed on Beaches Blue 1 and 2 followed by RCT24, the Division Reserve. 2/25 and 1/25 landed on Yellow 1 and 2. RCT 25 achieved much of its O-1 Line objectives, but RCT23 meet heavy resistance fighting through Charan Kanoa and failed to gain Mt Fina Susu. All of the 14th Marines landed on D-Day, but howitzer losses were high. Most of XXIV Corps Artillery (BGen Arthur M. Harper) landed on the Blue beaches on D+1 and 2. The largest tank attack the Marines would experience was launched pre-dawn on June 17 by some 44 mostly medium tanks. Over half were destroyed by just after dawn by 1/6 and 2/2.

The 16,404-man (plus 3,800 attachments) 27th InfDiv (MajGen Ralph C. Smith) was the Expeditionary Troops Reserve. It was released to VAC on the night of D+1. RCT165 landed that night on the Blue beaches and was attached to 4th MarDiv. RCT105 landed on the Yellow beaches on the 17th. Both fought to the island's south end. The Division Artillery landed on June 17 and initially was under the control of XXIV Corps Artillery. The Division HQ took charge of its regiments on the morning of the 18th. RCT106, both the Expeditionary Troops and Division Reserve, landed on June 20.

The 2d MarDiv continued to clear its zone while the 4th MarDiv fought toward the east coast, reaching it on the 18th. It then reoriented north on the 20th to the east of the 2d MarDiv. Both divisions then pushed north. On the 22nd the 27th InfDiv took up position between the 2d and 4th MarDivs and the push into central Saipan began. The Army division lagged behind, exposing the Marine divisions' interior flanks. This resulted in the relief of the commander by Marine LtGen Smith and his replacement by MajGen Sanderford Jarman on the 24th. The push north continued on the 27th. By this time units were mixed between divisions.

Saipan's broad central width was such that all regiments had to be placed in the line. Only a battalion served as the division reserve. The VAC Provisional Battalion was formed from VAC HQ and Corps Troops personnel on June 22 as a Corps Reserve. Shore Party personnel were formed into the Provisional Battalion, 2d MarDiv on June 24 to support 2/2 and served as a Division Reserve as no replacements had arrived. It then supported CT8 until dissolved in early July.

The 2d MarDiv was pinched out of the line on the 30th as the island narrowed. On July 6 the 27th InfDiv too was pinched out with the 4th MarDiv clearing the north end. Saipan was declared secure at 1615, July 9. Maniagassa, an islet in Tanapag Harbor, was seized on July 13 by 3/6. An unheard-of 1,780 Japanese troops surrendered and over 14,000 civilians were interned. Unfortunately large numbers were killed, with many committing suicide.

2d MarDiv	27th InfDiv	4th MarDiv
2d Marines	105th Infantry (-1st & 2d Bn)	23d Marines
6th Marines	106th Infantry	24th Marines
8th Marines	2d Bn, 165th Infantry	165th Infantry (-2d Bn)
1st Bn, 29th Marines		1st Bn, 105th Infantry
NTLF Reserve	**Saipan Garrison Force**	
25th Marines	2d Bn, 105th Infantry	

Tinian

Three miles to the south of Saipan lies Tinian (Tearaway). The gently rolling island, over 80 percent covered by sugarcane, is 10.25 miles long and five miles wide across the center. Its highest elevation was a 580ft hill and ridge mass on the south end. The 564ft Mt Lasso dominated the north end. The island was edged with 6–100ft cliffs with few suitable landing beaches.

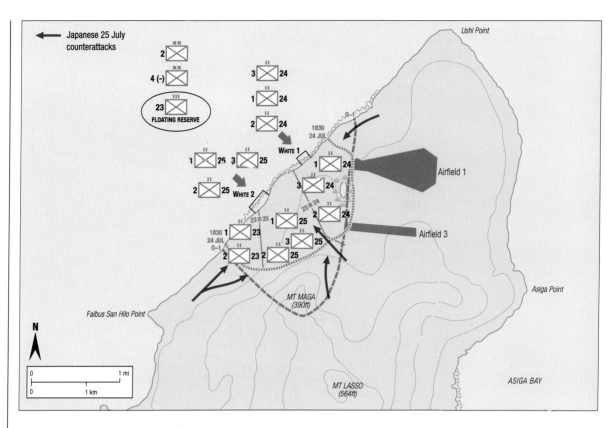

Tinian, J-Day, July 24, 1944.

The reinforced 50th Infantry, 29th Division defended Tinian with 5,050 troops along with 4,100 56th Guard Force IJN personnel. Four airstrips were located on the island. Some 18,000 Japanese civilians lived on Tinian, mostly in Tinian Town on the southwest coast.

Preparations for Tinian began when the 4th MarDiv assembled in rest areas on July 14, but the operation order was not given until the 17th. J-Day for the shore-to-shore assault was set for July 24. The 4th MarDiv would lead the assault followed by 2d MarDiv. Numerous 2d MarDiv elements were initially attached to the 4th to give it 21,618 men. Prov HQ, Amphibian Tractors, VAC was attached to 4th MarDiv with 539 LVTs, 68 LVT(A)s, and 130 DUKWs. The total landing force was 42,290 troops, of whom 35,055 were Marines.

The 4th MarDiv had lost almost 1,000 dead and 5,000 wounded on Saipan. The 2d MarDiv had suffered 1,300 dead and 5,000 wounded. Only 1,200 replacements for both exhausted divisions arrived prior to the Tinian assault.

V Amphibious Corps (Northern Troops and Landing Force)
VAC HQ&S Battalion (-)
VAC Amphibious Reconnaissance Battalion
Companies D and E, VAC Medical Battalion
VAC MT Company (-)
VAC Signal Battalion (-)
VAC Prov Engineer Group
18th and 121st NC Battalions

(continued on page 82)

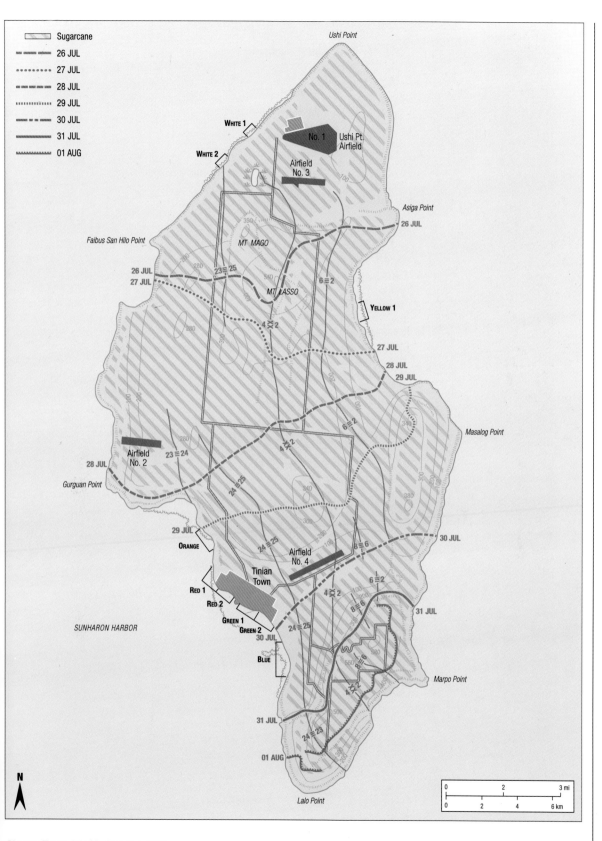

Legend:

- Sugarcane
- 26 JUL
- 27 JUL
- 28 JUL
- 29 JUL
- 30 JUL
- 31 JUL
- 01 AUG

Ushi Point

WHITE 1

WHITE 2

No. 1
Ushi Pt.
Airfield

Airfield
No. 3

Asiga Point

26 JUL

Faibus San Hilo Point

MT MAGO

390

26 JUL
27 JUL

23 ≡ 25

MT LASSO

540

6 ≡ 2

YELLOW 1

380

4 ⊠ 2

300

27 JUL

28 JUL
29 JUL

380

6 ≡ 2

Masalog Point

340

28 JUL

Airfield
No. 2

23 ≡ 24

4 ⊠ 2

Gurguan Point

24 ≡ 25

340

300

29 JUL

ORANGE

24 ≡ 25

Airfield
No. 4

30 JUL

8 ≡ 6

RED 1

Tinian
Town

6 ≡ 2

RED 2

4 ⊠ 2

100

GREEN 1

8 ≡ 6

31 JUL

GREEN 2

SUNHARON HARBOR

24 ≡ 25

30 JUL

BLUE

560

III 6

Marpo Point

4 ⊠ 2

31 JUL

24 ≡ 23

500

01 AUG

N

0		2		3 mi
0	2	4	6 km	

Lalo Point

Clearing Tinian, July 25–August 1, 1944.

34th Engineer Combat Battalion (USA)
HQ, Northern Troops and Landing Force Shore Party
17th AAA Battalion
7th Field Depot (-) (Reinforced)
3d Marine Ammunition Company (-)
18th, 19th, and 20th Marine Depot Companies
31st and 38th Medical Field Hospitals (USA)
96th, 97th, and 98th Medical Portable Surgical Hospitals (USA)
477th Transportation Corps Amphibian Truck Company (-)

The 27th InfDiv remained on Saipan as the VAC Reserve prepared to embark with four hours' notice. Its 105th Infantry and 1/29 remained on Saipan to conduct mopping up. Bombardment of Tinian began on June 11, before the Saipan assault, and continued through that action. A week after the landing 13 US artillery battalions on the south end of Saipan were shelling Tinian with 168 tubes. XXIV Corps Artillery was reorganized under the below structure on July 15 to control all 155mm guns and howitzers, and initially, all 105mm howitzers. The 105mm and 155mm howitzers (except two batteries of 106th Battalion) relocated to Tinian beginning July 27. The 155mm guns remained on Saipan as they could range all of Tinian.

XXIV Corps Artillery (USA)
HQ and HQ Battery, XXIV Corps Artillery (USA)
Groupment A [105mm]
HQ&S Battery, 10th Marines
3d and 4th Battalions, 10th Marines
3d and 4th Battalions, 14th Marines
4th 105mm Artillery Battalion, VAC
Groupment B [105mm]
HQ and HQ Battery, 27th InfDiv Artillery (USA)

Tinian Island viewed from the north. The two WHITE Beaches on which the Marines landed are on the lower right coast opposite Airfield No. 1, the large light-colored area. The circle at the left end of the airfield is a taxiway. Airfield No. 3 is the smaller light area just above No. 1.

(continued on page 83)

WHITE 2

WHITE 1

Airfield No.1

104th, 105th, and 249th Field Artillery Battalions (105mm Howitzer)
Prov Amphibian Truck Company, 27th InfDiv [DUKW]
Groupment C [155mm]
HQ and HQ Battery, 420th Field Artillery Group (USA)
2d Battalion, 55th Coast Artillery Regiment (155mm Gun) (Mobile) (USA)
32d Coast Artillery Gun Battalion (155mm Gun) (USA)
106th Field Artillery Battalion (155mm Howitzer), 27th InfDiv (USA)
145th and 225th Field Artillery Battalions (155mm Howitzer) (USA)
2d 155mm Howitzer Battalion, VAC (USMC)

The Navy preferred the landing to be on the wide beaches at Tinian Town (Orange, Red, Green, Blue) to ease cargo unloading. They were heavily defended as were the Yellow beaches on the northeast shore. The Marines preferred the White beaches on the upper northwest shore. The use of these beaches was unparalleled as White 1 was 65yds wide and White 2, 1,000yds southwest of White 1, was 160yds—far narrower than preferred for even company landing sectors much less a division. Flanked by low cliffs and coral outcroppings, the beaches were weakly defended. Scout-swimmers checked the beaches and currents and the Marines felt it was possible to achieve complete surprise.

The landing force embarked from Tanapag Harbor and Beaches Blue, Yellow, and Red on the night of July 23. The 2d MarDiv conducted a demonstration off of Tinian Town on the morning of the 24th while the 4th MarDiv launched its LVTs. The 2d MarDiv (- CT8) was the Northern Troops and Landing Force Reserve until landed on J+1. Of the 415 amtracs employed, 225 were Army.

4th MarDiv (Reinforced)
Regimental Landing Team 25
25th Marines (Reinforced)
708th Amphibian Tank Battalion [LVT(A)1/(A)4] (USA)
773d Amphibian Tractor Battalion (Reinforced) [LVT(2)] (USA)
2d Battalion [pioneer] Battalion, 20th Marines [shore party]
Company A, 4th Tank Battalion [M4A2]
Detachment, Company D (Flamethrower), 4th Tank Battalion [M3A1/M5A1]

(continued on page 84)

Company E, 2d Battalion, 24th Marines, with six LVT(A)4 amphibian tanks in the lead, makes its run in eight LVT(4)s toward Tinian's Beach White 1 on J-Day.

Company A, 1st Battalion [engineer], 20th Marines

Two platoons, Company D, 2d Armored Amphibian Tractor Battalion [LVT(A)4]

Detachment, 4th MT Battalion

Collection Section, Company A, 4th Medical Battalion

1st Platoon, 4th MP Company

Detachment, 1st Joint Assault Signal Company

Section, 1st Prov Rocket Detachment

Forward Observer Detachment, 14th Marines [artillery]

1st Band Section

Regimental Landing Team 24

24th Marines (Reinforced)

1st Battalion, 8th Marines

2d Armored Amphibian Tractor Battalion [LVT(A)4]

2d Amphibian Tractor Battalion (Reinforced) [LVT(2)/(4)]

1341st Engineer Combat Battalion (USA) [shore party]

Company B, 4th Tank Battalion [M4A2]

Detachment, Company D (Flame), 4th Tank Battalion [M3A1/M5A1]

Detachment, HQ&S Battalion, 20th Marines [engineer]

Company B, 1st Battalion [engineer], 20th Marines

Detachment, 4th MT Battalion

Collection Section, Company B, 4th Medical Battalion

2d Platoon, 4th MP Company

Detachment, 1st Joint Assault Signal Company

Section, 1st Prov Rocket Detachment

Forward Observer Detachment, 14th Marines [artillery]

2d Band Section

Regimental Landing Team 23 (Division Reserve)

23d Marines (Reinforced)

10th Amphibian Tractor Battalion (-) [LVT(2)]

Company C, 11th Amphibian Tractor Battalion [LVT(2)]

Company C, 4th Tank Battalion [M4A2]

Detachment, Company D (Flamethrower), 4th Tank Battalion [M3A1/M5A1]

Company C, 1st Battalion [engineer], 20th Marines

Detachment, 4th MT Battalion

Collection Section, Company C, 4th Medical Battalion

3d Platoon, 4th MP Company

Detachment, 1st Joint Assault Signal Company

Forward Observer Detachment, 14th Marines [artillery]

3d Band Section

Division Artillery

14th Marines (artillery) (-)

1st and 2d Battalions, 10th Marines [artillery]

1st and 2d Marine Amphibian Truck Companies

Division Engineers

20th Marines [engineer] (-)

(continued on page 85)

Support Group

    HQ Battalion, 4th MarDiv (-)

    2d Tank Battalion [M4A2/M3A1/M5A1]

    4th Medical Battalion (-)

    4th MT Battalion (-)

    4th Tank Battalion (-)

    4th Service Battalion

    Marine Observation Squadron 4

    1st Joint Assault Signal Company (-)

    Prov HQ, Amphibian Tractors, VAC

        5th Amphibian Tractor Battalion (-) [LVT(4)]

        534th Amphibian Tractor Battalion (-) [LVT(2)/(4)] (USA)

        715th Amphibian Tractor Battalion (-) [LVT(2)/(4)] (USA)

Beach WHITE 1 at high tide, on Tinian. The usable beach was 60yds wide and fronted by a 50yd-wide coral reef. The small Japanese defense detachment was located in crevasses and caves around the beach and the dense brush to its rear.

RCT24 landed on WHITE 1 at 0747 in the order of 2d, 1st, and 3d battalions in a column of companies. 3/25 and 2/25 landed abreast in company columns on WHITE 2 with 1/25 following. RCT23 (floating reserve) landed on WHITE 2 along with 1/8 to serve as the Division Reserve when all three CTs were in the line. The units pushed inland quickly, which was essential to provide room for the following troops and supplies, and soon closed the gap between the beaches. Some 15,600 troops were ashore the first day.

On J+1, 2d Tank Battalion, after landing with 4th MarDiv, was released to 2d MarDiv. Here an M4A2 of Company C supports the 8th Marines clearing Ushi Point, located on Tinian's north end and to the northeast of the WHITE beaches.

2d MarDiv (Reinforced)

Combat Team 2

    2d Marines (Reinforced)

    Company A (-), 1st Battalion [engineer], 18th Marines

    2d Prov Rocket Detachment (-)

    Collecting Section, Company E, 2d Medical Battalion

    Graves Registration Section, S&S Company, 2d Service Battalion

    1st Band Section

Combat Team 6

    6th Marines (Reinforced)

    Company B (-), 1st Battalion [engineer], 18th Marines

    Collecting Section, Company D, 2d Medical Battalion

    2d Band Section

Combat Team 8

    8th Marines (Reinforced) (- 1/8 until J+1)

    Company C (-), 1st Battalion [engineer], 18th Marines

    Collecting Section, Company C, 2d Medical Battalion

    Detachment, 2d Prov Rocket Detachment

    Graves Registration Section, S&S Company, 2d Service Battalion

    3d Band Section

Support Group

    HQ&S Company, 18th Marines [engineer]

    HQ Company, 1st Battalion [engineer], 18th Marines

        4th Platoon, Company B, 1st Battalion, 18th Marines

    2d Battalion [pioneer], 18th Marines (+ 4th Platoon, Company A and 4th Platoon, Company C, 1st Battalion, 18th Marines)

    HQ Battalion, 2d MarDiv

    2d Medical Battalion (-)

    2d MT Battalion (-)

    2d Service Battalion (-)

    2d Joint Assault Signal Company (-)

Division Troops initially remaining on Saipan

    Detachment, HQ&S Company, 2d Medical Battalion

    Companies B and C (-), 2d Medical Battalion

    Security detachment from each unit to guard equipment

The south end of Tinian, between Marpo and Lalo points, featured its most rugged terrain, with coral cliffs over 400ft high. The caves and crevasses in the rocky slopes were home to hundreds of Japanese troops and civilians.

On the morning of July 25 (J+1) CT8 landed on WHITE 1 and was initially attached to 4th MarDiv and regained its 1/8. It was followed by CT2 at noon. 2/6 landed on WHITE 2, but the rest of CT6 did not land until J+2. Most 2d MarDiv units attached to the 4th MarDiv were returned on J+2. The 2d MarDiv took over the east portion of the line and the 4th the west. The offensive resumed on the 25th and rolled south, gaining the island's tip on August 1 when Tinian was declared secure at 1855.

Marine casualties had been relatively light, fewer than 2,300, because of the operation's intentionally slow pace and the mass of forces and fire support. Prisoner counts are conflicting, one being 250 and another 400, possibly owing to confusion with Japanese civilians. Over 13,000 civilians were interned with approximately 4,000 killed.

Tinian and Saipan were developed into massive airbases to bomb Japan into submission. The 2d MarDiv remained on Saipan doing extensive mop-up until it departed for Okinawa in March 1945 as a floating reserve. It soon returned and remained until deploying to Japan in September. The 4th MarDiv remained on Tinian mopping up and was sent to Maui, TH in mid-August to prepare for the Iwo Jima assault.

Marine Commanders, Saipan and Tinian	
Expeditionary Troops, Fifth Fleet and V Amphibious Corps	
Commanding General	LtGen Holland M. Smith
	MajGen Harry Schmidt (VAC only from 12 Jul)
Chief of Staff	BGen Graves B. Erskine
Note: Commanding general, chief of staff, and G-1/C-1 for both commands were double-billeted. The G-2/C-2, G-3/C-3, and G-4/C-4 were different officers.	
VAC Troops	
VAC HQ&S Battalion	Maj Thomas R. Wert
VAC Amphibious Reconnaissance Battalion	Capt James L. Jones
VAC Medical Battalion	LCdr William B. Clapp (USN)
VAC Signal Battalion	Col James H. N. Hudnall
2d Armored Amphibian Tractor Battalion	LtCol Reed M. Fawell, Jr.
2d Amphibian Tractor Battalion	Maj Henry G. Lawrence, Jr. (to 2 Jul)
	Maj Fenlon A. Durand
5th Amphibian Tractor Battalion	Capt George L. Shead
10th Amphibian Tractor Battalion	Maj Victor J. Croizat
11th Amphibian Tractor Battalion	Maj Walter S. Haskell
2d Separate Engineer Battalion	LtCol Charles O. Clark
2d 155mm Howitzer Battalion	LtCol Narvin H. Floom
4th 105mm Artillery Battalion	LtCol Douglas E. Reeve
7th Field Depot	LtCol Edwin D. Partridge (to 25 Jun)
	Col Earl H. Phillips
XXIV Corps Artillery	BGen Arthur M. Harper (USA)
2d Marine Division	**MajGen Thomas E. Watson**
Assistant Division Commander	BGen Merritt A. Edson
Chief of Staff	Col David M. Shoup
2d Marines	Col Walter J. Stuart
1st Battalion	LtCol Wood B. Kyle

(continued on page 88)

2d Battalion	LtCol Richard C. Nutting
3d Battalion	LtCol Arnold F. Johnston (WIA 16 & 21 Jun)
	Maj Harold Throneson (to 5 Jul)
	LtCol Arnold F. Johnston (to 11 Jul)
	LtCol Walter F. Layer
6th Marines	Col James P. Risely
1st Battalion	LtCol William K. Jones (WIA 15 Jun)
2d Battalion	LtCol Raymond L. Murray (WIA 15 Jun)
	Maj Howard J. Rice (WIA 15 Jun)
	LtCol William A. Kengla (15 Jun only)
	LtCol Edmund B. Games
	Maj LeRoy P. Hunt, Jr. (to 11 Jul)
3d Battalion	LtCol John W. Easley (WIA 15 Jun)
	Maj John E. Rentsch (to 3 Jul)
	LtCol John W. Easley (KIA 2 Aug)
	Maj John E. Rentsch
8th Marine	Col Clarence R. Wallace
1st Battalion	LtCol Lawrence C. Hays, Jr. (WIA 15 Jun)
2d Battalion	LtCol Henry P. Crowe (WIA 15 Jun)
	LtCol Lane C. Kendall
3d Battalion	LtCol John C. Miller (WIA 15 Jun)
	Maj Stanley E. Larsen (WIA 15 Jun)
	LtCol Gavin C. Humphrey (from 10 Jul)
10th Marines [artillery]	Col Raphael Griffin
1st Battalion	Col Presley M. Rixey (to 24 Jun)
	Maj Wendell H. Best (to 16 Jul)
	LtCol Donovan D. Sult
2d Battalion	LtCol George R. E. Shell (WIA 16 Jun)
	Maj Kenneth C. Houston (to 16 Jul)
	Maj David L. Henderson
3d Battalion	Maj William L. Crouch (KIA 7 Jul)
	Maj James O. Appleyard (to 16 Jul)
	LtCol William C. Capehart
4th Battalion	LtCol Kenneth A. Jorgensen
18th Marines [engineer]	LtCol Russell Lloyd (to 24 Jun)
	Col Cyril W. Martyr
1st Battalion [engineer]	LtCol August L. Vogt
2d Battalion [pioneer]	LtCol Chester J. Salazar
3d Battalion [NCB]	Cdr Lawrence E. Tull (USN)
HQ&S Battalion, 2d MarDiv	Maj Melvin A. Smith
2d Medical Battalion	LCdr Claude R. Bruner (USN)
2d MT Battalion	Maj Milton J. Green
2d Service Battalion	Maj Edward V. Dozier
2d Tank Battalion	Maj Charles McCoy
Prov Battalion, 2d MarDiv	Maj Francis X. Beaner

 (continued on page 89)

4th Marine Division	**MajGen Harry Schmidt (to 11 Jul)**
	MajGen Clifton B. Cates
Assistant Division Commander	BGen Samuel C. Cumming
Chief of Staff	Col William W. Rogers
14th Marines [artillery]	Col Louis G. DeHaven
1st Battalion	LtCol Harry J. Zimmer (KIA 25 Jul)
	Maj Clifford B. Drake
2d Battalion	LtCol George B. Wilson, Jr.
3d Battalion	LtCol Robert E. MacFarlane
4th Battalion	Maj Carl A. Youngdale
20th Marines [engineer]	LtCol Nelson K. Brown
1st Battalion [engineer]	Maj Richard G. Ruby
2d Battalion [pioneer]	Maj John H. Partridge
3d Battalion [NCB]	LCdr William G. Byrne (USN)
23d Marines	Col Louis R. Jones
1st Battalion	LtCol Ralph Haas
2d Battalion	LtCol Edward J. Dillon (WIA 6 & 9 Jun)
3d Battalion	LtCol John J. Cosgrove, Jr. (WIA 19 Jun)
	Maj Paul S. Treitel
24th Marines	Col Franklin A. Hart
1st Battalion	LtCol Maynard C. Schultz (KIA 16 Jun)
	Maj Robert N. Fricke (to 27 Jun)
	LtCol Otto Lessing
2d Battalion	LtCol Richard Rothwell (to 23 Jul)
	Maj Frank E. Garretson (to 27 Jul)
	LtCol Richard Rothwell
3d Battalion	LtCol Alexander A. Vandegrift, Jr. (WIA 29 Jun)
25th Marines	Col Merton J. Batchelder
1st Battalion	LtCol Hollis U. Mustain
2d Battalion	LtCol Lewis C. Hudson, Jr.
3d Battalion	LtCol Justice M. Chambers (WIA 22 Jun)
	Maj James Taul (to 23 Jun)
	LtCol Justice M. Chambers
1st Battalion, 29th Marines	LtCol Guy E. Tannyhill (WIA 17 Jun)
	LtCol Rathvon McC. Tompkins (WIA 2 Jul)
	Maj William W. McKinley (to 15 Jul)
	LtCol Orin K. Pressely
Special & Service Troops, 4th MarDiv	Col Orin H. Wheeler
HQ&S Battalion, 4th MarDiv	LtCol Melvin L. Krulewitch
4th Medical Battalion	LCdr George W. Mast (USN)
4th MT Battalion	LtCol Ralph L. Schiesswohl
4th Service Battalion	Col Richard K. Schubert
4th Tank Battalion	Maj Richard K. Schmidt

Lessons learned

The lessons learned at Tarawa were invaluable: they were considered by many to have justified the controversial and costly assault, and were soon applied. Communications were a major problem. More reliable, waterproof radios were needed to maintain contact between units, particularly at lower echelons.

One of the most important changes in amphibious warfare was the use of amtracs to land assault troops. The introduction of gun-armed amtracs, already under development at the time of Tarawa, helped suppress beach defenses, such as those that had inflicted a heavy toll on Tarawa's reefs. Gun, rocket, and mortar-armed fire-support landing craft were also commissioned to provide even greater suppressive capabilities.

Manmade and natural obstacles could not be dealt with by these means, but needed to be located and either marked or destroyed in order to allow LVTs and landing craft to access the beaches. The only effective way to accomplish this was by using frogmen from the Navy's UDTs.

Bazookas, flamethrowers, and demolition techniques were essential to overcome Japanese inland defenses. This resulted in an increase from 24 to 243 flamethrowers and the allocation of a demolition kit to each squad. Training in the use of these weapons increased. Flamethrowers were also mounted on tanks and LVTs.

One of the most valuable lessons regarded the use of naval gunfire. Much was learned about the best projectiles and fuzes to use on different targets, and how best to attack them. The same applied to close air-support tactics. The control of

Marine and Army infantry battalion participation

Island/group	Marine Corps	Army
Gilberts	9 (Tarawa)	4 (Butaritari)
New Britain	9	2*
Marshalls	9 (Roi-Namur)	9 (Kwajalein)
	3 (Eniwetok)	2 (Eniwetok)
Saipan	19	9
Tinian	18	–

* Nine 40th InfDiv battalions relieved 1st MarDiv.

Marine casualties, Southwest and Central Pacific

Operation	KIA	DOW	WIA	MIA	Total
Tarawa	904	93	2,233	88	3,318
New Britain	276	66	948	133	1,423
Roi-Namur	175	31	617	181	1,004
Eniwetok	181	38	568	39	826
Saipan	2,077	367	8,575	708	11,727
Tinian	300	65	1,921	3	2,289

artillery, naval gunfire, and air support demanded close attention and much was done to refine this. Not only were request and control procedures developed, but special units were organized strictly for this purpose.

The use of smoke-screens during landings also provided some important lessons. Delivered by bombers, smoke was used for the first time on Cape Gloucester, New Britain. Although opposed by the Marines, the Navy's decision to use it prevailed: the result was that it drifted across the beach and boat lanes. Aggressive boat handling and the lack of opposition prevented it from hampering the landing, but it could have obscured the beaches and blinded coxswains, resulting in landing on the wrong beach, disarray in boat formations, and collisions. Smoke and dust from the pre-landing bombardment was considered sufficient to blind the enemy. From this point onwards, its use to screen landings was more carefully planned.

The 75mm pack howitzer, although prized for its light and compact nature, left much to be desired in terms of its effectiveness. By the end of the Marianas campaign many recommended that it be replaced by the 105mm, which it eventually was.

Tarawa and other period operations confirmed the need for medium tanks rather then the relatively ineffective light models. Most light tanks were replaced by medium Shermans by late-1944. Tank–infantry coordination and training were greatly improved, as were small-unit tactics for defeating pillboxes. Tactical training was made even more realistic and demanding.

The introduction of new weapons and equipment led to an increase in specialist training. BAR men, mortar men, and machine-gunners, for example, were not just infantry given additional training, but dedicated specialists trained specifically on their main weapon.

The importance of realistic and extensive rehearsals covering all aspects of a landing was reinforced. However, time constraints often precluded this, and rehearsal locations similar to the objective island were not always available.

A radio operator transmits Morse code on a TBX portable radio while an assistant hand-cranks the power generator. Under ideal conditions it could transmit up to 30 miles, but in hilly, jungle terrain this was usually much less. It would eventually be replaced by the Army's SCR-284.

Chronology

1943

16 August	4th MarDiv activated at Camp Pendleton, CA.
25 August	PhibCorpsPacFlt redesignated VAC at Camp Elliott. Troop Training Unit, Amphibious Training Command, PacFlt established at Camp Elliott to provide training to Marine and Army divisions.
1 November	Tactical Group 1, VAC formed in Hawaii.
20 November	2d MarDiv assaults Tarawa Atoll.
26 December	1st MarDiv assaults Cape Gloucester, New Britain.

1944

21 January	5th MarDiv activated at Camp Pendleton, CA.
31 January	4th MarDiv assaults Roi-Namur.
17 February	Tactical Group 1 assaults Eniwetok.
22 February	Task Group A, IMAC formed on Guadalcanal.
6 March	5th Marines assaults Volupai-Talasea, New Britain.
20 March	Task Group A occupies Emirau.
15 April	IMAC redesignated IIIAC on Guadalcanal.
19 April	1st Prov MarBde formed on Guadalcanal.
5 June	FMFPac established as type command for Marine forces in the Pacific Ocean Area.
15 June	VAC with 2d and 4th MarDivs assaults Saipan.
21 July	IIIAC with 3d MarDiv and 1st Prov MarBde assaults Guam.
24 July	VAC with 4th and 2d MarDivs assaults Tinian.
6 September	IIIAC with 1st MarDiv assaults Peleliu.
7 September	6th MarDiv activated on Guadalcanal.

MajGen's Thomas E. Walton, 2d MarDiv (left) and Clifton B. Cates, 4th MarDiv (in an undershirt) coordinate the advance of their divisions as they push toward southern Tinian.

Bibliography

Alexander, Joseph H. *Utmost Savagery: The Three Days of Tarawa* (Annapolis, Naval Institute Press, 1995)

Crowl, Philip A. *US Army in World War II, The War in the Pacific: Campaign in the Marianas* (Washington, DC, US Government Printing Office, 1955)

Crowl, Philip A. *US Army in World War II, The War in the Pacific: Seizure of the Gilberts and Marshalls* (Washington, DC, US Government Printing Office, 1955)

Frank, Benis M. and Shaw, Henry I., Jr. *History of US Marine Corps Operations in World War II: Vol. IV, Central Pacific Drive* (Washington, DC, US Government Printing Office, 1966)

Graham, Michael B. *Mantle of Heroism: Tarawa and the Struggle for the Gilberts, November 1943* (Novato, CA, Presidio Press, 1997)

Heinl, Robert D., Jr. and Crown, John A. *The Marshalls: Increasing the Tempo* (Washington, DC, HQ Marine Corps, 1954)

Hoffman, Carl F. *Saipan: The Beginning of the End* (Washington, DC, HQ Marine Corps, 1950)

Hoffman, Carl F. *The Seizure of Tinian* (Washington, DC, HQ Marine Corps, 1951)

Hough, Frank O. and Rentz, John R. *The Campaign of New Britain* (Washington, DC, HQ Marine Corps, 1952)

Hoyt, Edwin P. *Storm over the Gilberts* (New York, Mason/Carter, 1978)

Miller, John, Jr. *United States Army in World War II. Cartwheel: the Reduction of Rabaul* (Washington, DC, Government Printing Office, 1959)

Morison, Samuel A. *History of US Navy Operations in World War II: Vol. 6, Breaking the Bismarcks Barrier, 22 July 1942–1 May 1944* (Boston, MA, Little, Brown and Company, 1950)

Morison, Samuel A. *History of US Navy Operations in World War II: Vol. 7, Aleutians, Gilberts and Marshalls, March 1943–April 1944* (Boston, MA, Little, Brown and Company, 1950)

Morison, Samuel A. *History of US Navy Operations in World War II: Vol. 8, New Guinea and the Marianas, March 1944–August 1944* (Boston, MA, Little, Brown and Company, 1953)

Rottman, Gordon L. *US Marine Corps Order of Battle: Ground and Air Units in the Pacific War, 1939–1945* (Westport, CT, Greenwood Publishing, 2001)

Rottman, Gordon L. *World War II Pacific Island Guide: A Geo-Military Study* (Westport, CT, Greenwood Publishing, 2001)

Shaw, Henry I. Jr. and Kane, Maj Douglas T. *History of US Marine Corps Operations in World War II: Vol. II, Isolation of Rabaul* (Washington, DC, US Government Printing Office, 1963)

Wright, Derrick *A Hell of a Way to Die: Tarawa Atoll, 20–23 November 1943* (London, Windrow & Greene, 1996)

A camera-equipped scout and observer searches for identification plates on a destroyed Japanese 75mm Type 41 (1908) regimental gun on New Britain. Analyzing the data on these plates provided technical information, the name and location of the manufacturer (used for air-raid targeting), and how many had been produced (by examining serial number ranges). Also, by comparing construction materials, refinements, and searching for manufacturing shortcuts an idea could be formed of the effect of air raids on production.

Abbreviations and linear measurements

AAA	anti-aircraft artillery		MP	Military Police
amtrac	amphibian tractor (see LVT)		MT	Motor Transport (aka "Motor-T")
Asst	Assistant		NCB	Naval Construction Battalion ("Seabees")
AT	anti-tank		NCO	non-commissioned officer
BAR	Browning Automatic Rifle		NGF	Naval gun fire
BLT	Battalion Landing Team		O-1 Line	Objective Line 1
Bn	Battalion		Prov	Provisional
Btry	Battery		RCT	Regimental Combat Team
Co	Company		Regt	Regiment
CO	Commanding Officer		S&S	Service and Supply (platoon/company/battalion)
CP	command post		SMG	submachine gun
CT	Combat Team		SNLF	Special Naval Landing Force (Japanese)
Det	Detachment		SPM	self-propelled mount (M3 halftrack-mounted
DOW	died of wounds			75mm gun)
FMF	Fleet Marine Force		TF	Task Force
FMFPac	Fleet Marine Force, Pacific		TG	Task Group
HMG	heavy machine gun		TH	Territory of Hawaii
HQ	Headquarters		T/O	Tables of Organization
HQMC	Headquarters, Marine Corps		US	United States
HQ&S	headquarters and service (company/battery)		USA	United States Army
IIIAC	III Amphibious Corps		USAAF	United States Army Air Forces
IJA	Imperial Japanese Army		USMC	United States Marine Corps
IJN	Imperial Japanese Navy		USN	United States Navy
IMAC	I Marine Amphibious Corps		VAC	V Amphibious Corps
InfDiv	Infantry Division (US Army)		WIA	wounded in action
JASCO	Joint Assault Signal Company		WO	Warrant Officer
JICPOA	Joint Intelligence Center/Pacific Ocean Area		XO	Executive Officer (second-in-command)
KIA	killed in action		(-)	less (elements detached from unit)
LCI	Landing Craft, Infantry		(+)	reinforced (additional elements attached)
LCT	Landing Craft, Tank			
LCVP	Landing Craft, Vehicle or Personnel		**Marine Corps officer ranks**	
LMG	Light machine gun		2dLt	2d Lieutenant
LSM	Landing Ship, Medium		1stLt	1st Lieutenant
LST	Landing Ship, Tank		Capt	Captain
LT	Landing Team		Maj	Major (USN LCdr, lieutenant-commander)
LVT	Landing Vehicle, Tracked ("amtrac")		LtCol	Lieutenant-Colonel
LVT(A)	Landing Vehicle, Tracked (Armored)		Col	Colonel
MarBde	Marine Brigade		BGen	Brigadier-General ("one-star")
MarDiv	Marine Division		MajGen	Major-General ("two-star")
MIA	missing in action		LtGen	Lieutenant-General ("three-star")

Distances, ranges, and dimensions are given in the contemporary US system of inches, feet, yards, and statute miles rather than metric:

feet to meters:	multiply feet by 0.3048
yards to meters:	multiply yards by 0.9144
miles to kilometers:	multiply miles by 1.6093

Index